Mastering Social Work Skills series

Edited by Jane Wonnacott

This series of short, accessible books focuses on the everyday key skills that social workers need in order to practise effectively and ensure the best possible outcomes for service users. Easy to read and practical, the books feature key learning points, practice examples based on real-life situations, and exercises for the reader to enhance their learning. The books in this series are essential reading for post-qualifying social work students and social work practitioners.

Jane Wonnacott is Director of In-Trac Training and Consultancy, UK.

MASTERING
Social Work Values and Ethics

Farrukh Akhtar
Foreword by Hilary Tompsett

Jessica Kingsley *Publishers*
London and Philadelphia

The bullet lists on pp.90–91 have been printed with kind permission from GSCC.
Table 4.1 on p.97 has been used with kind permission from
Nikki Owen and Audience with Charisma Ltd, 2011.
Figure 5.1 on p.112 has been used with kind permission from Oxford University Press.
Figure 5.5 on p.123 has been used with kind permission
from the National Association of Social Workers.

First published in 2013
by Jessica Kingsley Publishers
73 Collier Street
London N1 9BE, UK
and
400 Market Street, Suite 400
Philadelphia, PA 19106, USA

www.jkp.com

Library of Congress Cataloging in Publication Data
Akhtar, Farrukh Nahid, 1966-
  Mastering social work values and ethics / Farrukh Nahid Akhtar.
     pages cm
  Includes bibliographical references and index.
  ISBN 978-1-84905-274-0 (alk. paper)
  1. Social service--Moral and ethical aspects. I. Title.
  HV10.5.A44 2012
  174'.93613--dc23
                                        2012041885

British Library Cataloguing in Publication Data
A CIP catalogue record for this book is available from the British Library

ISBN 978 1 84905 274 0
eISBN 978 0 85700 594 6

CONTENTS

Figures and Tables

Foreword

As Chair of JUC SWEC (Joint University Council Social Work Education Committee) I am very aware that social work programmes, students and practitioners will be thinking how they can engage with the social work reforms in qualifying social work education and practice and in very changing contexts.

This book presents in a very readable and practical format an introduction to values and ethics across the professional lifespan and taking account of organisational contexts. It will be of particular value to new social work students meeting the new requirements (Health and Care Professions Council [HCPC] Standards of Proficiency/Code of Conduct, Performance and Ethics, and The College of Social Work's Professional Capabilities Framework [PCF]). It will also be relevant to practitioners looking for material to assist them with reflections on practice as they prepare for re-registration with the new regulator (HCPC) and think about their careers in relation to the PCF.

The interplay between the 'personal and professional' highlights that social workers bring their own beliefs, attitudes and spirituality to the consideration of issues, while also seeking to develop informed and systematic approaches to improving their understanding and professional judgements. Key to this is the ability to reflect critically, a skill which is helpfully developed through the practice related case studies, matrices for analysis, up to date contextual material, which integrates the new requirements and standards, each chapter also contains key theoretical perspectives and useful tips that will help direct practitioners to further resources and tools to support professional development, self-management and well being in relation to caseload demands, dealing with stress, and direct practice challenges.

This book will provide a valuable new text in the literature of values and ethics and stimulate readers to explore wider and complementary texts dealing with some of the theoretical dimensions in more depth or detail.

Professor Hilary Tompsett
Kingston University and St George's, University of London

Series Editor Foreword

When social workers have confidence in their own skills, purpose and identity, and in the system in place to back them up, they have a huge amount to offer. They collaborate effectively with other professionals and adapt to new roles and expectations. Most importantly, they forge constructive partnerships with people who find themselves vulnerable or at risk and make a sustained difference in their lives.

(Report of the Social Work Task Force 2009, p.5)

This book forms part of a series which aims to increase social work confidence through exploring the essential skills that social workers need to do their job, and to give accessible, practical ideas based on evidence from research and practice.

The series challenges the view that social work is about 'doing the simple things well', a view that has taken hold in some circles since the publication of the Laming report in 2003. Social work is not simple; it is a complex activity, and social workers are working with risk and uncertainty on a day to day basis.

It is the premise of this series that good social work involves the capacity to develop and maintain relationships, manage the emotional dimension of the work and make judgements and decisions often in the light of conflicting information. This is demanding work and will only be effective if social workers are encouraged to reflect critically on their practice and continually develop their knowledge and skills. Too often the time for reflection and skill development is minimal, and social workers rely on prescriptive procedures which do not always assist the creativity and critical thinking which is fundamental to good, safe practice.

The starting point for authors of this series is a positive expectations model, which is based on the premise that social workers want to do a good job and need flexible tools and frameworks to help them practise within the challenging environment within which they work. The authors are experienced social work trainers and practitioners, and the content of each book is based on material that has been extensively tested with front line practitioners and their managers.

A comment on the title

The series has been entitled 'Mastering Social Work' as it aims to move beyond basic skills to those which may support the practitioner in more challenging circumstances. 'Mastering' is a process of developing expertise by applying learning and knowledge to practice. It is a continuous activity. Our aim and hope is that this series will assist social workers in this task by providing ideas and frameworks to support them in their day to day work.

Mastering Social Work Values and Ethics

This important book in the series tackles ethical dilemmas that are at the heart of social work practice, yet may feel hard to articulate in the fast pace of day to day work. Dilemmas such as weighing up the right of a person to independence versus ensuring their safety from harm, or deciding the point at which a parent can no longer provide adequate care for their child do not generally pose simple questions with clear cut answers. Instead they involve the interplay of a range of tangible and less tangible factors in the decision making process. These dilemmas can be multiplied when resources are scarce and social workers are being directed by their employers in a way that does not fit neatly with their own beliefs and values. Moving towards social work practice which recognises the impact of the sometimes messy and complex world of feelings, beliefs, attitudes and values may feel impossible in pressured environments yet is vital for the well being of both the practitioner and service users alike. For example, social workers who are struggling with dissonance between their own beliefs and values and the expectations of their organisation are likely to experience extreme anxiety. Unless ways are found to understand and work with this emotion, practice may be compromised or a potentially valuable member of staff lost to the social work profession. The frameworks and tools in this book provide a means whereby social workers and their managers can name and reflect on the ethical issues inherent in the work, and develop self-awareness and the supportive environment necessary to maximise outcomes for users of social work services.

ACKNOWLEDGEMENTS

My thanks to colleagues at Kingston University, in particular to Keith Davies, Nigel Elliot and Robert Stanley for continuing to be an inspiration in many respects, but especially in the depth of their knowledge about ethics; to Alix Walton (Royal Holloway, University of London) for acting as a powerful mentor and role model.

Thanks also to Colette Elliott-Cooper, Yvonne Cochrane, Meral Mehmet, Emense Tulloch, Usha Chauhan and Naveed Bokhari whose social work experience and practice wisdom is second to none.

Finally, a warm thanks to each and every member of my family, for their continued unconditional love and support. It sustains me in everything I do.

Introduction

The unexamined life is not worth living.

(Socrates, cited by Plato in 'Apology')

The above quote is part of a speech made by the Greek philosopher Socrates in the year 399 BCE. He was defending himself against charges of corrupting youth and not believing in the gods that were recognised by the state. He denied these claims, calmly reiterating his belief about free thought and free speech. When the charges against him were upheld and he was told that his punishment was death, Socrates calmly accepted this decision and his fate. To some, he may represent the epitome of living (and dying) according to one's values.

This may seem a rather sobering start to a book about mastering social work values and ethics, but there are parallels here with social work. Practitioners enter the profession because they want to make a positive difference to the lives of vulnerable people. However, in doing this, they may have to grapple with some of their most deeply held values. At times, they may have to act within the law and according to statute (and the wishes of the state) but outside their own personal value base.

For example, can removing a child from an abusive situation be justified? Most practitioners would argue it is. Is it still justified if it leads to further trauma for the child – in the form of inappropriate placements; losing contact with friends, siblings and extended family; becoming unable to engage in formal education; becoming emotionally and financially dependent on the local authority?

Some practitioners may argue that organisational procedures, the law, courts and managment make decisions about removing children from their families. Social workers simply implement those decisions. Others may argue that social workers work with the information they have available at the time and try to achieve the best outcome they can with the resources available. All of these perspectives are valid and hold some truth. They can also be used as a screen to hide behind, to evade thinking about or connecting with the unease of carrying out the unenviable tasks that society has allocated for social workers. Tasks such as: deciding if someone is so ill that they warrant treatment against their wishes, or that they lack the capacity to make their own decisions or manage their own finances, or are not a 'good enough' parent and so have lost the right to bring up their own children.

In the demands of everyday practice, it is understandable that the work itself has priority. Somehow, the ethical dilemma of a particular case or specific situation can be lost as the next crisis takes over. There is a danger that workers can lose touch with important aspects of themselves, of important personal values. If left unattended, this neglect can turn to disillusionment, leading to the oft-quoted, 'This is not why I came into social work.' The choice may seem to be about leaving social work, or remaining in a profession that does not resonate with one's most fundamental and deeply held beliefs. Over two thousand years later, Socrates' position may have taken on mythical proportions, but the challenge of working consciously within one's ethics and values in social work is a very real one.

This book provides exercises to enable practitioners to reflect upon their practice and some of the moral and ethical dilemmas they may face, and to develop strategies to remain connected to the values that brought them into social work, and that will, we hope, enable them to not only remain in the profession, but continue to thrive as a practitioner.

Chapter 1 sets out the context of values and ethics within social work, presenting a value matrix that encapsulates the key dimensions. Chapter 2 provides an overview of seminal ethical theories and their relevance to social work and presents a matrix of ethical theories that summarises the links between theory and the kinds of questions that are asked in social work practice. These two matrices are referred to throughout the book.

Chapter 3 explores how professional values can evolve over time, and the impact this can have on practice. Chapters 4 and 5 look at the ethical dilemmas of working with service users, especially in direct work with them. Chapter 4 explores professional boundaries, the use of power and the way decisions are made, while Chapter 5 offers tools to develop self-awareness in practitioners. Finally, Chapter 6 considers ethical issues within a team and organisational context.

A common theme to emerge in the coming pages is that of reflective practice, of making decisions in a mindful way that acknowledges a practitioner's multiple accountabilities – to service users, managers, the wider organisation and, of course, oneself. This last point is often forgotten. Work that focuses on good practice, in a client focused way, by necessity involves putting aside one's own values. But it was those very values that brought people into social work in the first place. The challenge, therefore, is to be able to find a way that enables workers to work effectively and within their own value base; to continue doing work that is meaningful and contributes to the worker's sense of well being. The tools and exercises presented in the following chapters will encourage practitioners to revisit and reevaluate their evolving values and to consider to what extent their practice remains ethical, according to their own standards.

CHAPTER 1

Setting the Context

Key messages

- Values and ethics are central to social work practice.

- Ethical practice needs to acknowledge the concept of 'complex accountability'.

- Understanding and referring to the values matrix is a useful way of keeping the connection between one's values and one's professional duties.

Two social workers were chatting over lunch. One spoke of a mentally ill sibling who had relapsed after receiving a letter from the Department of Works and Pensions, who were reviewing his capacity to work. 'Every day is already such a struggle for him. The thought of losing the one thing that gives him some independence and dignity was just too much for him.'

Her colleague considered this and her thoughts wandered to her elderly mother. 'Yes,' she replied, 'Living in her own home gives my mum a huge sense of dignity. Your brother is lucky to have your support. I wonder how someone without any support would cope?' The discussion then moved on to the service users that they were both working with, and the likely impact that such a letter would have on them.

How would you describe the values that were being articulated by each of the social workers in this scenario?

Introduction

This chapter looks at the context of values and ethics in social work. The friends in the above scenario did not decide to sit down and discuss 'social work values'. They were catching up with each other's news. Nevertheless, their conversation highlights their values and can serve as a useful way to locate the place of values and ethics within social work.

First, the workers' views demonstrate their beliefs about vulnerable people and how they should be treated. Their conversation shows the subtle interplay between the personal and the professional. In this situation, the beliefs about promoting a family member's right to independence and self-determination mirrors what they would want for service users. In other situations, there may be more of a discord between personal and professional values. For example, there may be situations when one's religious or spiritual beliefs clash with one's duties – such as in euthanasia. You may believe that terminally ill people have the right to end their own lives but, as a professional, you cannot support it.

Second, although legislation and policy are not explicitly referred to in the scenario, there is a sense of these workers being aware of a 'system' (in this case, a benefits system) within which services are provided. Social workers are often the conduit for determining what social care services someone may be entitled to. If that person does not meet specific criteria, they will not be eligible for the service. The fact that social work is generally a publicly funded activity, carried out 'at the instigation of the state and on behalf of society' (Clark 2000, p.78) is also a contributing factor. The service user's eligibility to access resources is dependent on how well they are funded and how high or low eligibility criteria have been set. In conducting such assessments, social workers can encounter a range of ethical issues, within and beyond their control. Chapter 6 explores further the ethical issues that practitioners face within their teams and the wider organisation, as they tackle such 'systems'. The discussion about the place of legislation within ethical practice continues later in this chapter.

Third, the way social workers respond to ethical issues needs to be within an anti-discriminatory and anti-oppressive framework that encompasses a critical reflection of the situation and an appropriate analysis of it. This, along with law, policy and an adherence to the professional codes of practice forms part of a matrix which places values at the centre of practice (see Figure 1.1). Values can be personal and professional. For some, there will be a distinctive difference between the two. For others, they may be very similar. No differentiation has been made in the matrix in this regard.

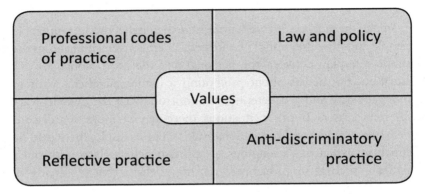

Figure 1.1 Values matrix

The value matrix is interactive, so any one aspect will be influenced by the others, and vice versa. For example, a 14-year-old girl is pregnant and asks her social worker for support to be able to see the pregnancy through to full term, without her parents knowing. Of course the social worker will have personal as well as professional views about abortion, especially if the mother happens to be a child herself. However, those values will be influenced by the worker's professional codes, by the legal framework, by the policies and procedures set by her workplace. These aspects are clearly defined and set a framework for practice.

Then there are other factors that may not be so rigid but may be just as powerful in influencing the worker's practice – such as the social location of the pregnant girl. She may be from a culture in which teenage pregnancies are more acceptable – such as Romany travelling families or, equally, she may be from a culture where this is frowned upon. It will be the worker's responsibility to reflect on such issues and to clarify what is and is not relevant in any decision that is made. In most cases, the action taken by the social worker will be the same, but the way they make sense of those actions, and their personal feelings about taking them, will be different from person to person.

Each aspect of this matrix will be discussed in turn. The basic premise of this chapter is that social work in hard times requires 'complex accountability' (Clark 2000, p.83) for practitioners, but this heightens rather than decreases the need to work in an ethically sound way. The term complex accountability refers to the fact that in any given situation, social workers can have a range of accountabilities; many of which can simultaneously clash. For example, there may be conflicting needs and priorities, such as between the pregnant girl and the rights of her unborn baby.

The values matrix forms one central element of this book and will be referred to from time to time.

Values matrix: Professional codes of practice

In April 2005 the title 'social worker' became protected in the UK and only qualified social workers who were registered as such could call themselves by it (Care Standards Act 2000). Up until July 2012 the body that registered practitioners (in England) was the General Social Care Council (GSCC). All social workers were required to have a social work qualification, to meet specific requirements around their continuing professional development, and were also required to demonstrate their ability to meet National Occupational Standards. In July 2012 the registration of social workers was transferred to the Health and Care Professions Council (HCPC) which issued *Standards of Proficiency: Social Workers in England.*

At the same time there were other changes that significantly altered the professional codes that social workers are expected to adhere to. This included the Social Work Reform Board's (SWRB 2011) recommendation about a Professional Capabilitiy Framework (PCF) that was accepted by the College of Social Work, which was established and became a legal entity in the same year. The PCF sets out nine different capabilities that develop, in ever increasing complexity, from the point of entering social work training, through to the Assessed and Supported Year in Employment (ASSYE), to becoming a qualified social worker, a senior social worker, an advanced practitioner, and beyond.

Arguably all of the nine capabilities relate more or less directly to social work values. However, four of these have an explicit reference to ethically based practice. These are 'values and ethics', 'diversity', 'rights, justice and economic wellbeing' and 'critical reflection and analysis'.

In addition to the above changes, 2012 also saw the British Association of Social Work (BASW) and the International Federation of Social Workers (IFSW) updating and amending their Code of Ethics (BASW 2012; IFSW 2012).

Whilst these are all codes relating to social work practice, there is an important distinction to be drawn between them. The HCPC's codes refer to 'proficiency' in practice for qualified social workers, whereas the PCF focuses on continually developing 'capabilities' throughout one's career, starting as a social work student. These two set of codes are very much about *standards* of practice. This compares with the BASW and IFSW codes which are specifically codes of *ethics*. These are statements, moral principles, based on the value base of the organisation.

Nevertheless, there are areas of commonality between all four bodies. First, all expect social workers to be able to critically reflect on their values and to be aware of the impact this could have on their practice; to be able to recognise ethical dilemmas and to work alongside service users, carers and other professionals in resolving them. Second, they state, on the one hand, that social workers should be able to promote service users' rights to autonomy and self-determination, whilst at the same time being able to balance this with their professional accountability or with legal requirements. Finally, where social workers feel that decisions have been made that are detrimental to service users, they are required to challenge those decisions.

Do social workers share a common professional ideology? Abbott (1998) identified social workers as having four key values:

1. respect for basic human rights

2. a sense of social responsibility

3. commitment to individual freedom

4. support of self-determination.

Further studies have replicated these findings (Abbott 2003; Greeno *et al.* 2007) and they are certainly supported by the IFSW and BASW in identifying human rights and dignity and social justice as important values in their Code of Ethics (BASW 2012; IFSW 2012). As already stated, the areas of diversity, of service users' rights, justice and economic well being have also been given greater prominence by the HCPC and in the PCF. But it remains to be seen whether these changes will impact on practitioners' ability to work to specific codes and to be able to balance this against working to their own personal ethical code, their personal sense of integrity.

Values matrix: Law and policy

One way of ensuring that workers practise ethically is for them to work within their organisational policy and within appropriate legislation. This provides a powerful context that sets the parameters of the work. However, there is also a danger of rules being followed in a rigid and an unthinking way. This is more likely to happen at times when organisational change is rapid.

The HCPC's second proficiency standard requires practitioners to 'be able to practise within the legal and ethical boundaries of their profession' (HCPC 2012, p.7).

However, between 2008 and 2012, for example, according to the government's own website (legislation.gov.uk), no less than 138 public general acts were passed by parliament. Not all of these were relevant to social workers and those working within the probation service. However, a significant number were. Some of these are listed in Table 1.1.

Table 1.1 Some of the 138 public general acts passed by parliament between 2008 and 2012

Children and Young People Act 2008	Charities Act 2011
	Education Act 2011
Criminal Evidence (Witness Anonymity) Act 2008	Police (Detention and Bail) Act 2011
Education and Skills Act 2008	Terrorism Prevention and Investigation Measures Act 2011
Autism Act 2009	
Welfare Reform Act 2009	Domestic Violence, Crime and Victims (Amendment) Act 2012
Child Poverty Act 2010	
Children, Schools and Families Act 2010	Health and Social Care Act 2012
	Legal Aid, Sentencing and Punishment of Offenders Act 2012
Crime and Security Act 2010	
Equality Act 2010	Protection of Freedoms Act 2012
Personal Care at Home Act 2010	Welfare Reform Act 2012

Points to consider

- How much of the legislation passed relates to your area of social work?

- Within your field, were there any pieces of legislation that you had not been aware of?

- Apart from training that you may receive through your employer, to what extent do you ensure you have a good working knowledge of all the relevant legislation relating to your post?

However fastidious you are, it is unlikely that you will be able to keep up to date with all the changes of law and the subsequent changes in policy and procedures within social work as a whole. Such is the pace of change. Change does not have to be bad, but even positive changes within an organisation can be unsettling and a huge source of stress. Typical reactions to legislative changes can be, 'I came into social work to help people, not to be an agent of the state' or, 'If only politicians would stop meddling and undoing what the last lot put in place, we might be able to get the job done…'

As any social worker worth their salt knows, legislation and policy are important. They give social workers the mandate, the authority to carry out their responsibilities. It is not in the remit of this book to discuss different pieces of law or policy and to refer to their moral or ethical context. Individuals form their own opinions on this. The main ethical issue about any law or policy that has to be implemented is how social workers can balance the rhetoric behind the act or policy versus the reality of implementing it?

The personalisation of social care is one example of this. This government initiative was announced in 2008 to encourage 'self-directed support' so that service users could manage their own personal budgets, individual budgets and direct payments. One perspective is that 'personalisation' is an enabling process that offers service users flexibility, autonomy and freedom. It could also be argued that this was indeed the rhetoric behind the policy but the reality for many local authorities was that 'personalisation' was used as an excuse to make severe cutbacks to existing services and to set up systems that were simply inadequate, such as limiting budgets so that even the most basic of services could not be purchased, thereby not giving service users any choice or autonomy at all.

With experience, and the right kind of support, social workers become adept at tackling such situations. Banks (2006) distinguishes between *ethical issues* (her example is deciding whether to issue a service user with a disabled parking permit); *ethical problems* (which may involve making a difficult moral decision, such as turning down the application for a parking permit for someone who does not quite fit the agency criteria) and *ethical dilemmas*, where a practitioner faces equally unwelcome outcomes whatever they decide (e.g. a service user needs a permit but does not fit the agency criteria. Should the practitioner 'bend' the criteria in this instance?).

Many ethical problems or dilemmas faced by social workers do not have clear answers. One way in which they respond to this is by practising within agency procedures; following the law or policy guidelines to the letter. However clear such guidelines are, they will not be able to tell practitioners what to do in every situation.

Following procedures 'on auto pilot' can also lead to emotional shut down, an unquestioning approach which acts as a defence against the difficult feelings generated when working constantly with vulnerable, needy people.

Simply focusing on procedures will not be enough to ensure good practice. As the interactive nature of the values matrix suggests, being mindful of discrimination and creating space to reflect on one's practice act as buffers against such approaches.

Values matrix: Anti-discriminatory practice

The next factor to be discussed on the values matrix is anti-discriminatory practice. As stated already, the matrix is interactive. It recognises that how anti-discriminatory practice is carried out will be affected by what legislation and organisational policies allow, by the professional codes, by one's ability to reflect on specific situations and make sense of them, as well as by one's personal and professional value base.

Anti-discriminatory practice is an approach that has its origins in the 1980s when there was an increasing awareness of the impact of racism in society. It is now used in a broader sense to include all socially based discrimination (such as discrimination on the basis of class, disability, age, sexuality or gender). The term 'anti-oppressive practice' is often used interchangeably with anti-discriminatory practice. For some there is no differentiation between the terms (Thompson 2012). Other practitioners (such as Dalrymple and Burke 2003) make a distinction between recognising discrimination and having an awareness of this in their work (working in an anti-discriminatory way) and working in an anti-oppressive way. They see the latter as a more proactive stance in acknowledging power differentials and structural inequality in society. These different interpretations can be seen as a reflection of writers' and practitioners' different value bases. Readers may wish to reflect on this and make up their own minds about their individual positions. Both terms will be used in this book. The term anti-discriminatory practice (ADP) is used around issues of discrimination and anti-oppressive practice (AOP) is used around issues of oppression.

Service users do not come in neat packages where 'isms' can be identified and worked with. Thompson (2012) refers to being aware of multiple oppressions that occur at a personal, cultural or structural (PCS) level.

Crenshaw (1993, p.1241) wrote about the difficulties of working with black women of different classes around issues of domestic violence. She referred to the different 'intersectional identities' of the women: the places where gender, race and class, as well as experiences of violence, met. The emphasis here is on recognising the importance of social location in defining some aspects of our experience, particularly at places where aspects of our identity (that wider society deems to be 'subordinate') may intersect with society.

In the United States social work academics, including Ortiz and Jani (2010), have built on the concept of intersectionality to develop critical race theory (CRT) within a social work context. The theory is built on the assumption that race is a social construction that 'exists primarily for the purpose of social stratification' (p.175) and permeates society's psyche. Although the theory was initially about race, it has subsequently been broadened out to include class, gender, sexual orientation, religion, ethnicity, disability, educational achievement and residential status. By having a commitment to social justice, and recognising the 'multiple subordinating identity variables' (p.175), it is argued that practitioners can work more proactively and holistically with service users, avoiding clichéd categorisations.

Simply recognising intersections in and of itself does not ensure anti-discriminatory practice, as each individual will interpret their social location according to their life experiences. Recognising dominant and subordinate identities (compared to the dominant group in society) enables a multi-layered picture to be formed. For example, a young black heterosexual man who is single and a qualified lawyer will have a different social location to a deaf white young man whose sexuality is unclear.

Practitioners are encouraged to work with service users, through a process of open inquiry, to encourage counter-storytelling – a process that captures their lived experience (as opposed to the stories or stereotypes held about them in wider society). It is social workers' responsibility to then reflect on the nature of the issues identified and how these relate to their own remit, to the services they can provide, and whether these services are culturally appropriate.

Critical race theory's emphasis on social justice fits in well with the professional capability of 'rights, justice and economic well being' (SWRB 2011). It is important that social workers understand the economic position of the people they work with. However, as Thompson and Thompson (2008) point out, this is about having a wider structural knowledge about how discrimination can occur at an institutional level to contribute to poor outcomes for some sections of society.

Points to consider

- What is your social location?
- What (if any) are your 'subordinate identities' and how do they 'intersect' with 'mainstream society'?
- What impact does this have on your identity, and how you live your life?

Anti-discriminatory practice relates to standards 5 (be aware of the impact of culture, equality and diversity on practice), 6 (practise in a non-discriminatory manner) and 8 (communicate effectively) of the HCPC standards of proficiency (HCPC 2012). The last of these is included because, for a practitioner to be able to communicate effectively, they need to be aware of the values they hold. These can come from their family, or the wider culture within their community, or they can be values that have been consciously cultivated over time – such as professional values.

One of the challenges of looking at one's values is their intangible nature. In her discussion about beliefs, values and inter-cultural communication, Robinson (2004) cites Hofstede's work in comparing value differences across 50 different countries. These findings are particularly transferable to societies with a diverse range of cultures and communities and are also explored in Chapter 3 of another book in this Mastering Social Work Skills series (Gast and Patmore 2012). Hofstede found that eight factors are important in communication across different cultures. A lack of awareness of these factors was likely to lead to erroneous assumptions being made about service users. This could then influence their assessment and decisions about possible intervention. The dimensions referred to were:

1. power-distance

2. uncertainty avoidance

3. individualism vs collectivism

4. masculinity

5. high and low context communication

6. immediacy and expressiveness

7. emotional and behavioural expressiveness

8. self-disclosure.

It is useful to briefly consider each, along with working examples.

Power-distance

This refers to the way in which different cultures view differences in status between people. Cultures that score highly on this will have clear rituals that define and maintain status differences between members. Cultures that score low on this may tend to minimise rules and customs, as well as status differences between members.

Case study

Andrew was supervising a student. He became increasingly impatient with her and judged her as 'submissive' because she tended to address people formally. Andrew's belief system looked upon people as equal, and so not requiring deference. He began to doubt his student's capacity to be assertive enough as a social worker because she seemed to 'look up' to authority so much. His student's belief system was that the young showed respect to those older than them, and to those in authority.

Uncertainty avoidance

This refers to the way that different cultures respond to uncertainty, particularly in times of stress and anxiety. Hofstede's *Dimensions of National Cultures in 50 Countries and Three Regions* (cited by Robinson

2004) found few gender differences. The emphasis was more on a cultural ability to respond to high levels of uncertainty, or not. Some cultures were more attuned to this than others.

Case study

Anka had suffered from depression since the birth of her two-year-old son, who had been born with profound physical and learning disabilities. The social worker assessing her was experienced in working with severe disabilities. She wondered if Anka's depression was about not having had a 'normal' child and felt that she should have come to terms with this by now. For Anka, a single parent, it was the uncertainty of her son's future that contributed to her mental fragility. She did not know, week to week, what services or support they would be entitled to, and she worried about who would care for him, if anything ever happened to her.

Individualism vs collectivism

A culture that promotes individualism will prioritise one's individual needs, hopes and aspirations over the collective needs of one's family, community or wider society. Both aspects can exist in all cultures, but cultures tend to prefer one over the other. In the UK, for example, cultures from African Caribbean or Asian origin could be seen as more collectivistic than mainstream white people of UK origin.

Case study

Krishna became a social worker in her fifties, after her own children had grown up and married. Her son continued to live with her in their family home, along with his wife. When she joined a disabilities team, she struggled with the concept of disabled adults 'living independently'. It seemed an expensive solution for the state, as well as an isolating one for service users. She simply could not understand why anyone would want to live alone. She eventually accepted that not all cultures and families were the same as her own.

Masculinity

This dimension refers to the extent to which gender-related differences are emphasised in society generally and specifically in work situations. Countries which score high on this include Japan, Austria and Italy, whilst countries that score the lowest include Denmark, Sweden and Norway. There may also be individual and cultural differences within countries, but the concept is useful in helping understand some domestic situations.

Case study

Suzanne struggled to assess the mental capacity of Mrs Okonkwo because her husband kept interfering in the assessment process. Suzanne could not work out if he was just trying to be helpful or if he was being controlling. She began to suspect some form of domestic abuse. Finally, the couple's adult daughter clarified things for her, explaining that her parents had always had very segregated roles, and her father saw himself as the 'man of the house' whose duty it was to represent his wife's best interests.

High and low context communication

This refers to the extent to which a message is limited to explicit verbal communication or includes more 'contextual' information, such as the wider circumstances around the event, including the social setting, the historical context, as well as non-verbal communication, gestures and tone of voice. Both levels of communication exist in all cultures, but one will tend to predominate.

Case study

Bernice worked in an intake and assessment team. The work was demanding and sometimes there was pressure to speed up interviews as there was a queue of people waiting to be seen. She noticed that some people took longer to tell her what the 'problem' was than others. It was as if they had a story to tell, and couldn't get to the heart of the matter without giving her a detailed narrative. She learned that there was no point cutting them short or trying to ask specific questions – that tended to throw them off track. It saved time in the long run, to enable them to tell their story, their way and then proceed with her questions.

Immediacy and expressiveness

This dimension measures the degree of closeness that people experience with each other. High scores on both factors will demonstrate psychological as well as physical closeness (immediacy) and strong expressions of warmth, touch, smiling (expressiveness). High ratings on both of these factors are signs of 'contact' cultures.

Case study

Maria's cousin was visiting from Colombia. They had been inseparable as children but had not seen each other since Maria's family had emigrated, when she was six. She had been looking forward to catching up with her cousin so much but, when they actually met, she found herself feeling uncomfortable, and suffocated. She felt her cousin was far too exuberant in her behaviour. It seemed unauthentic and 'over the top'. She sat too close to her for comfort and had an annoying habit of reaching over and pressing her arm. Maria was not 'touchy-feely' and just wanted to run away.

Emotional and behavioural expressiveness

This dimension refers to thoughts and feelings and how they are communicated to others. Some cultures (such as African Caribbean) can be seen as too emotionally expressive when compared to the stereotype of white British reserve. This expressiveness can be experienced by others as antagonistic; for example, the negative stereotype of the aggressive, hostile black male whose anger seems out of proportion with a situation.

Case study

Doug and Jenni were travelling home after an evening out. The bus was quite full. The only voice to be heard was of a Rastafarian who was speaking loudly on his mobile phone, about his car breaking down.

'Why does he have to shout, and say the same thing over and over again?' Doug asked, in exasperation. Jenni was not sure how to reply. She intuitively knew the man was not shouting, but was simply venting his frustration in his own way.

Self-disclosure

Individuals vary in their inclination to talk about themselves, or their private lives. However, this dimension refers to one's culturally based willingness to discuss such information. Hofstede's research (cited in Robinson 2004) indicates, for example, that European Americans are more prone to disclosing personal information than African Americans.

Case study

Aiguo's mother had passed away several years ago. He had come to admit that the physical care of his father (who was now 95) was proving increasingly difficult. A neighbour had persuaded him to contact social services. Aiguo was horrified at the intrusive nature of the questions that were asked of him. He felt that social worker was being disrespectful and insensitive.

As the above examples show, a lack of awareness of some of these dimensions, and of their impact on communication, could lead to social workers making culturally biased assumptions about the people they are working with. Whatever the social location of the practitioner, they may make the assumption that their world view is the 'correct' one and that, by default, the service user is lacking in some respect. This could skew their assessment of the situation and have huge negative repercussions.

Anti-discriminatory practice involves being mindful of one's own social location, as well as others; of issues of 'sameness' with service users and of issues of 'differences'. This will be explored in more detail in Chapter 5. Being mindful in this way requires the ability to reflect on one's practice. That forms the fourth part of the values matrix.

Values matrix: Reflective practice

Whilst the significance of practising reflectively may be apparent, it may not be automatically clear to readers why this forms the final part of the values matrix. This will be discussed after reflective practice has been defined.

The need for social workers to be able to reflect on their practice is well documented (Munro 2011). Social workers are told they need to be more 'analytical' in their assessments, that they need to 'critically reflect' or be 'critically reflexive' in their approach, or just more 'critical'. These terms are used interchangeably, as if they mean the same thing. Social workers may have a sense of being asked to do something but there may be confusion as to what this is and how to do it.

The three main approaches that tend to be defined are reflective, reflexive and critical practice. Proponents of each will vouch that their model allows for the greatest learning. Jones (2009) differentiates between them, whilst acknowledging that, in practice, the differences are not so clear. All three processes involve analysing a situation and trying to learn from it. She argues that reflexive practice enables greater awareness of moral dilemmas and therefore allows practitioners to challenge others, as well as their own practice.

D'Cruz, Gillingham and Melendez (2007) differentiate between critical reflection and critical reflexivity. To them, critical reflection involves reflecting on something that is in the past. It involves thinking about a critical incident or event and learning lessons from this, which may be generalisable to other situations. On the other hand, critical reflexivity is much more about a present situation and involves taking a stance which may lead to insights or awareness of how things could be different around that situation. A practitioner begins by identifying hidden assumptions that they made in a critical incident, and then relate this to how they could think or practice differently. This learning may not be readily generalisable to other situations. Fook and Askeland's work (2007) is of particular note here, in promoting reflexivity as a working concept.

Another helpful way of looking at these differences is presented by Brechin (2000) who map the three domains of critical practice as 'critical action', 'critical reflexivity' and 'critical analysis'. They break these down into guiding principles. Critical analysis involves evaluating the practitioner's existing knowledge base (whether that is theory, policy or practice) and acknowledging the different perspectives that are available. It involves thinking about them at different levels, in an ongoing way, not just as a one-off event. This leads to critical action where the practitioner uses their skills in a purposeful way, acknowledging power imbalances, to empower service users.

These differences can be confusing. The term used in this book is reflective practice, as it assumes that any analysis must include a critical element that considers one's own assumptions, values and power base. Reviewing these provides an alternative perspective that can challenge existing practice (Thompson and Thompson 2008).

Most practitioners agree about the importance of reflective practice and will declare that they perform their duties in this way. Perplexingly, workers can be apparently competent, with a sound knowledge of policy and law and good report writing skills, but they may not be able to locate *themselves* within their practice, or reflect on what they do in any meaningful way. Two examples spring to mind – both of experienced, qualified practitioners who had built up a strong reputation within their organisations of being 'good' workers. The first was fast heading into a career as a manager and had cut himself off from any emotional connection to his work so that all he could relate to were the procedures and timescales that had to be adhered to, and that earned him so much praise. The second was a worker who refused to discuss racism, because she practised in London, which was so diverse that 'racism did not exist'. She dealt with 'diversity issues' because they were boxes that had to be filled in during assessments.

Lord Laming criticised this 'tick box' approach in his report on the protection of children in section 3.15 of his report:

Reflective practice

The role of social work staff and managers is particularly critical in ensuring enabling action to protect children. There is concern that the tradition of deliberate, reflective social work practice is being put in danger because of an overemphasis on process and targets, resulting in a loss of confidence amongst social workers. It is vitally important that social work is carried out in a supportive learning environment that actively encourages the continuous development of professional judgement and skills... (Laming 2009, p.32)

Points to consider

- How do you define 'reflective practice'?
- How do you evaluate your skills in this area?

A theme to emerge from the above discussion is for the need to link one's 'self' to one's practice. This may be being aware of one's personal or professional values, one's emotional response to a situation and a willingness to explore what this may mean. Social work involves establishing relationships with others. This cannot happen when workers are on 'auto pilot'. Indeed, to say that it leads to dangerous practice may be an understatement.

Social workers are expected to 'demonstrate an ability to reflect on and analyse [their] own experience (educational, personal, formal and informal)' from the point they enter into social work training onwards. This is under 'Critical reflection and analysis', one of the capabilities in the Professional Capabilities Framework (SWRB 2011, p.3).

The HCPC proficiency standards that this relates to are:

9.9   Work with resistance and conflict.

9.10   Understand the emotional dynamics of interactions with service users and carers.

11   Be able to reflect on and review practice.

11.1   Understand the value of critical reflection on practice.

14   Gather, analyse, critically evaluate and use knowledge to make recommendations or modify practice.

(HCPC 2012)

BASW (2012) takes this further in its statement of ethical principles, by linking reflective practice with value 2.3: Professional Integrity: making considered professional judgements:

> Social workers should make judgements on balanced and considered reasoning, maintaining awareness of the impact of their own values, prejudices and conflicts of interest on their practice and on other people. (BASW 2012, p.10)

Aptly, this brings us back to values and their centrality in social work. This is an issue that is revisited many times throughout this book.

Conclusion

This chapter has explored the context of values and ethics in social work and has done so using the values matrix (see Figure 1.1). It has argued that values and ethics are central to social work practice and interact at all levels of practice, but particularly in how workers meet their professional responsibilities in relation to the professional codes of practice, in their implementation of law, and organisational policy, in their understanding and practice of anti-discriminatory practice and in the way they are able to reflect and analyse their actions and the impact of them on service users. All this takes place within the context of 'complex accountability' (Clark 2000, p.83).

The next chapter will look at ethical theories and their impact on practice.

Further reading and resources

BASW (2012) provides the current codes of practice for the British Association of Social Workers.

Beckett and Maynard (2009) would be useful to practitioners wishing to explore values and ethics from an anti-oppressive perspective.

Clifford and Burke (2009) would be useful to practitioners wishing to explore values and ethics from an anti-oppressive perspective.

Disbennett (2007) 'The Values Game' is a fun and insightful way to get a clearer sense of the values that are important to you. It can be accessed at www.coachlee.com/valugame/LongList.html.

HCPC (2012) gives the HCPC standards of proficiency.

IFSW (2012) provides the International Federation of Social Workers code of ethics.

Hofstede, G. 'Dimensions of National Cultures in 50 Countries and Three Regions.' In Robinson, L. (2004) 'Beliefs, Values and Intercultural Communication.' In M. Robb, S. Barrett, C. Komaromy and R. Rogers (eds) *Communication, Relationships and Care: A Reader.* London: Routledge, Taylor and Francis.

SWRB (2011) gives the Social Work Reform Board's Professional Capability Framework.

CHAPTER 2

Ethical Theories

Key messages

- Understanding ethical theory is key in making informed ethical decisions.

- Whatever individual practitioners' position is regarding religion or spirituality, they need to ensure they are 'spiritually literate'.

- The matrix of ethical theories is useful in mapping and thereby clarifying ethical issues in practice.

> Are morally good acts willed by God because they are morally good, or are they morally good because they are willed by God?
>
> (Socrates, cited by Plato
> in 'Euthyphro', 380 BCE)

Introduction

This chapter provides an overview of key ethical theories, discusses their relevance to social work and explores the nature and extent of professional values and their impact on the social work task.

Since time began, humanity has tried to make sense of its existence. As the above quote indicates, it is difficult to know what came first, an innate morality, or humanity's construction of it. Howe (1999, p.21) refers to this need to understand and make sense of our world, as the 'search for the true, the good and the beautiful'. By this, he means science, ethics and aesthetics. Science is seen as 'the true' as it seeks to understand the world of nature, including human nature. Ethics is 'the good'; it seeks out principles by which we should live, to order our lives. Aesthetics is 'the beautiful'. It is the search for balance and harmony in our lives.

Our focus is on 'the good'. Ethical theory has its origins in philosophy, which means the love of wisdom. This was a school of thought preceding and also having a wider remit than scientific inquiry. Thompson (1995, p.56) describes it as a 'framework for explaining and understanding aspects of the world and of our experience'. Even today, the emphasis is on logical reasoning.

There are three different types of ethical theory (see Figure 2.1). Normative ethics is the study of ethical theory and principles. This section of the book will focus on normative ethics in that it will be looking at the different ethical theories. Applied ethics seeks to identify the morally correct course of action by using philosophical methods. The remaining chapters of this book will look at different practice issues for social workers and will return to these ethical approaches, to see if they can offer a useful way to understand the issues. Metaethics, or analytical ethics, seeks to understand the nature of moral terms and judgements. This is beyond the scope of this book.

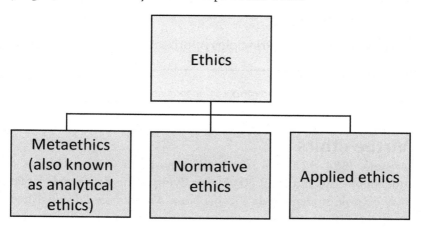

Figure 2.1 Ethics and ethical theory

Figure 2.2 shows the main types of theory that have influenced the western world, and social work, in particular. These will be discussed in turn. Goodwin (1993) notes that these theories are preoccupied either by what one *ought* to do in a specific situation, or by what action will achieve the 'greatest good'. They can, however, be difficult to understand and to locate within a contemporary context. For this reason, the theory will first be described within its original context, with reference to contemporary/modern philosophers, as appropriate. This will be followed by a discussion about how it relates to social work.

The ancient Greeks had a huge influence on ethical theory, so it is fitting to begin our journey with Aristotle, the founder of virtue ethics.

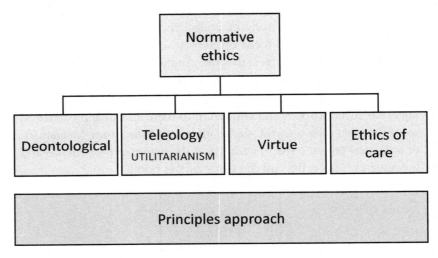

Figure 2.2 The main ethical theories within normative ethics

Virtue ethics

Aristotle (384–322 BCE) was born in northern Greece. He was a student of Plato and spent 20 years studying for his degree, a fact that may console students today. In his book *Nicomachean Ethics* (written in about 350 BCE), he saw ethics as being concerned with everyday practical issues, such as how one can live a 'good' or 'virtuous' life.

For Aristotle, this involved acquiring good habits and developing a good character. He coined the term *eudaimonia* which means happiness or well being and is the optimum activity for the human soul. Twelve key moral virtues were identified, which he felt were essential for this. They were: courage, temperance, liberality, munificence, high-mindedness, right ambition, good temper, friendliness/civility, sincerity, wittiness, modesty and just resentment. Each virtue had a 'moral mean', an optimal balance. Underdeveloping or overindulging this balance led to imbalances of character. For example, the virtue of 'friendliness or civility', if underdeveloped, could result in aloofness. If in excess, it could lead to sycophantic behaviour.

The emphasis was on developing one's character so that it would result in a better society. Each citizen was deemed to have a responsibility to do this and to fully participate in the community, even at a political level. This was a time when people regularly voted on all manner of things – including whether or not they should go to war. It was clearly understood that if the people voted yes, it was the people themselves who would be doing the fighting in any battle.

Aristotle believed in the best jobs for the best people, not based on ancestry or privilege. He saw it as each individual's responsibility to develop themselves to their optimal virtues.

Modern-day virtue ethicists include Alasdair MacIntyre (1985) who proposes a refocusing on virtues as a way of society reclaiming its moral compass. The idea of individuals developing their characters fits in well with many religions, as well as with modern ideas about spirituality and personal development.

However, unlike other ethical theories, virtue ethics does not provide answers to specific moral dilemmas. Lists of virtues can have limited value. Who decides what can and cannot be included? Should one similarly have lists of characteristics that should be avoided? Another limitation of virtue ethics is that it is impossible to see behind a virtuous character, to the intention of the person concerned, which may be far from virtuous.

Virtue ethics: Relevance to social work

A virtue ethicist may ask the following questions in relation to social work:

- What makes a good social worker?

- What are the qualities that social workers need to practice and develop in order to become excellent workers?

- How do you get the best people for the best jobs in social work?

Making up long lists of characteristics may not provide the answer to these questions. However, there are some key characteristics that most people would agree are essential in a good social worker, such as an ability to communicate and to empathise with service users. It could also be argued that the Professional Capability Framework (PCF) (SWRB 2011) is one way of doing just this. This sets out the capabilities needed by social workers, from the point they enter social work training, through to their Assessed and Supported Year in Employment (ASSYE), to being an experienced social worker, an advanced practitioner and beyond. The PCF has been designed as a way of representing standards of practice within social work. This explicit requirement around social workers and their continuing professional development shows how a virtue ethics approach is still relevant today.

A common criticism of social workers from service users is that they are not clear enough in what changes they expect. Virtue ethics promotes practitioners in assessing the character, willingness and ability of service users to change, to develop the characteristics needed to live independently (e.g. to what extent is it worth building a case for this person to go into drug rehab? How likely are they to be able to stop misusing drugs? Will this young person leave the gang they are a part of and change their offending behaviour?). What virtue ethics cannot do is assist social workers in making a decision about service users who do not have the capacity to make these changes.

Deontology

We move on from the ancient Greeks, to the Prussian town of Konigsberg (now in Germany), where Immanuel Kant (1724–1804) lived and founded deontology. In the 80 years of his life Kant never travelled more than ten miles beyond his native home town (Lewis 2005). This did not stop him from becoming one of the most influential philosophers of our time.

As O'Neill notes:

> His writings on ethics are marked by an unswerving commitment to human freedom, to the dignity of man, and to the view that

moral obligation derives neither from God, nor from human authorities and communities, nor from the preferences or desires of human agents, but from reason. (O'Neill, cited in Singer 1993, p.175)

The '*deon*' in deontology means 'duty'. The '*logos*' refers to 'the science of'. Kant was interested in how morals can be gained from pure reason. An action was either correct or not, due to its inherently moral nature. One did something, not because it was the virtuous thing to do (as Aristotle would argue) or because of its consequences (as utilitarianism would argue), but because it was the right thing to do, on that occasion and on every occasion. It was important for Kant that moral laws were 'universalisable'. Something could not be called a law unless it was a universal concept. He made many such 'formulations' and referred to them as 'categorical imperatives'. These included:

1. Act in such a way that your actions ought to be 'universalisable'.

2. Treat people as ends in themselves and never solely as a means to an end.

3. Act in such a way as you would have others act towards you.

Kant formulated his ideas in his book *Groundwork for the Metaphysics of Morals* in 1785. It can be seen that these principles are just as relevant today. His core theme of treating others as you would want to be treated does have a universal resonance.

However, there is also a rigidity in deontology that does not lend itself to areas of complexity. Kant gives the following scenario for us to consider: you are at home when there is a knock on the door. An angry, vehement man stands there, brandishing a knife. He is looking for a friend of yours (who lies sleeping peacefully inside). He asks if your friend is inside. How would you respond?

For Kant, lying under any circumstances was unacceptable. For him, a moral person always acted out of duty alone. Every citizen had a duty to speak the truth. If everyone lied, society could not function. Therefore it was a moral obligation to always speak the truth.

Modern day deontologists include W. D. Ross (1930), who was considered a pluralist deontologist, in that he believed that there are a number of general duties that we all need to uphold (such as not lying, not harming others) and that when conflicts arise, our intuitive judgement enables us to discern which duty has the priority.

Deontology: Relevance to social work

Kant lived in austere times and this is reflected in his theory. However, there are important aspects of his thinking that have permeated into the very foundations of social work. The most fundamental of these is the focus on values which is present in four out of nine of the PCFs (SWRB 2011) namely: values and ethics; diversity; rights; justice and economic well being; and critical reflection and analysis. These have been already discussed in Chapter 1. As was mentioned, the fundamental value about each person having respect and dignity in their own right is of Kantian origin. It could also be argued that this value is faith based, as is Kant's categorical imperative about treating others as you would have them treat you.

Another aspect of deontology that remains relevant to social work is the emphasis on duty. Social work continues to answer the call of helping the most vulnerable people in society by acting as a safety net to those who otherwise would suffer significant harm. Although social workers today would probably not regard themselves as agents of morality, in many respects their tasks and priorities are guided by the legal mandate, which is in effect the moral framework that society has defined for them.

Social workers are frequently faced with moral dilemmas and may have to make choices that are unwelcome, whatever the outcome (Banks 2006). Similarly, in deontology, rules can be rigid. Kant offers no trade-offs between one's different obligations and says nothing about what to do when one's obligations clash, as in the earlier scenario.

Utilitarianism

Utilitarianism is a theory that originates in a broader school of thought: teleology. '*Telos*' means root or end purpose. The focus of any action is not whether it is the right thing to do because it is moral, but on what the likely outcomes will be. Consequentialism is an offshoot of this. Utilitarianism is a theory that was built on the foundations of teleology and consequentialism. It was founded by the eccentric British legal philosopher Jeremy Bentham (1748–1832) and was then further developed by the son of one of his students, John Stuart Mill (1806–1873). Bentham outlined his ideas in *The Principles of Morals and Legislation* in 1789. Pleasure and pain were seen as key motivators. One wanted more of the former and to completely avoid the latter. This became the 'utility principle' – the rightness or wrongness of any action was determined by how useful it was, in extending the greatest happiness for the greatest number of people.

Bentham went so far as to create a formula (his hedonic calculus) to calculate what to do when faced with a moral dilemma. This included considering factors such as the intensity of the issue, its duration, the likely resulting sensations (pleasure or pain) and the likely number of people that would be affected (Bentham 1789).

Mills went on to build on this work by referring to the harm principle – each individual can behave as he or she wishes, as long as their actions do not harm anyone (including themselves). He also distinguished between *act* and *rule* utilitarianism. The former applied to individual acts – so each time an act was carried out, one had to evaluate if doing so would result in the greatest happiness for the greatest number, whereas rule utilitarianism offered general rules to offer the greatest happiness for society.

If we consider the example of lying, act utilitarians would consider each situation. It may be for the greatest good to lie in some situations (e.g. to avoid hurting another's feelings over an unsuitable gift). Rule utilitarians would argue that generally, for society to function there needs to be some honesty in people's transactions with each other and so would uphold telling the truth as a general rule.

Modern day utilitarians include Peter Singer (1993), who has written much about rights – animal as well as human. He has added a third type: *preference* utilitarianism. This involves an equal consideration of each person's preferences but does not imply that everyone has 'equal rights or should be treated equally, but that each should be treated in a way that is appropriate' (Thompson 2010, p.84).

Utilitarianism: Relevance to social work

Utilitarianism emerged at a time of scientific and social revolution. In many respects, what it proposed at the time was also revolutionary. This was a theory about and for the people. It espoused human rights. It said that women and gay people were equal to men, and that their happiness should also count in the consideration of the greatest good. Mill published *The Subjection of Women* in 1869, becoming one of the first supporters of feminism. Bentham also supported the abolition of slavery, and of physical punishment.

This mirrors the value base in social work today, which advocates for 'justice, rights and economic well being' (SWRB 2011, p.3), as well as being 'aware of the impact of culture, equality and diversity on practice' and practising in a 'non-discriminatory manner' (HCPC 2012, p.9).

There are times when social workers need to make difficult decisions and base these on the possible consequences, not in the next hour or few days, but in a service user's lifetime. Social workers tend to be acutely aware of the 'harm principle' which is embedded in social work values, and in legislation.

Utilitarianism does have it limitations. According to the theory, dog fighting should have at least an equal status in terms of 'culture' to say, poetry, as at one time more people would have participated in the former than the latter. However, Mill argued that pleasures of the mind were of a higher order than physical pleasures (Mill 1863). This seems to contradict his own theory and raises the point that happiness is purely subjective and not an easy thing to measure. It also questions the extent to which the theory can challenge power differentials in society.

With respect to social work, practitioners can be faced with difficulty around defining what is acceptable within specific cultural and legal limits and in protecting the rights of the minority. For example, should the fact that female genital mutilation is common in some cultures mean that it should be legalised in the UK? Or is the current legislation (Female Genital Mutilation Act 2003) correct in offering protection to a relatively small number of its citizens?

So far, the discussion around ethical theory and social work has focused on classical theories that have stood the test of time. The discussion now moves on to more modern paradigms that nevertheless offer useful perspectives to add to the social worker's ethical theory toolkit.

Ethics of care

Most mainstream ethical text books will not discuss the ethics of care as an ethical theory but, as will be seen, from a social work perspective it has an important place alongside more traditional theories. The founder of the approach is Carol Gilligan. She focuses on the caring relationship and how this task is usually carried out by women, along with specific responsibilities.

Gilligan (1993) initially wrote in response to research that was being carried out by Lawrence Kohlberg (1984), on how morality develops throughout the lifespan. Kohlberg's approach was to present his subjects with a series of scenarios and ask them their views on the ethical dilemmas that were presented. From this he formulated a stage theory detailing how morality evolves. Gilligan became critical of Kohlberg's approach.

This was because the majority of his early research had been carried out on boys, and because Gilligan felt that Kohlberg had failed to acknowledge differences in the way boys and girls made sense of social situations. An often quoted example is Kohlberg's scenario of Heinz, a man whose sick wife would inevitably die unless she received some medicine. Heinz was unable to afford the full cost. The question put to the boys was: should he break in to a chemist and steal the medicine?

Gilligan repeated the same experiment with a mixed sample and found that girls tended to score very differently to boys. They tended to focus on aspects of 'care' and relationship (e.g. that Heinz should go and try to speak to the chemist again and negotiate a payment plan with him) while boys focused on aspects of 'justice' (the moral rightness or wrongness of stealing) (Beckett 2002). She called this difference the 'ethics of care'.

In its broadest sense, the theory focuses on the vulnerable in society, who are in need of care, and the people providing that care. Gilligan focuses on the caring relationship and how this task is usually carried out by women, along with the specific responsibilities it entails. 'What an "ethic of care" requires is to relate the need on an emotional level, a consideration lacking in deontology and consequentialism' (Parrott 2010, p.64).

Ethics of care: Relevance to social work

Ethics of care's focus on the vulnerable in society has an immediate relevance to social work, along with its emphasis on the caring relationship.

However, some feminists argue that rather than increasing awareness of women's devalued positions in society, ethics of care reinforces these social divisions. Gilligan argues that the ethics of care highlights the interdependent nature of the caring relationship and the importance of attending to the *context* of any caring situation. This is something that social workers would agree with. Caring is a multi-faceted task. Assumptions can easily be made. The oppressed can also be the oppressor – such as an elderly parent who financially abuses their adult daughter with learning disabilities, who is acting as their full time carer. Unravelling some of these complexities lies at the heart of good practice.

Another criticism of this approach is that it fails to give guidance about what one should do in any given situation. For social workers, working with uncertainty every day, this may not be so relevant. Standard 9 of the HCPC's (2012) Standards of Proficiency focuses on working appropriately with others to promote individual growth, development and independence whilst standard 12 is about ensuring the quality of one's practice.

Beauchamp and Childress: Principles approach

Beauchamp and Childress' book *Principles of Biomedical Ethics* (2009) is now a seminal text book for nursing and medical practitioners. Their approach has become known as the 'principles' approach. Banks (2006) notes that this is based on a concept of common morality of ordinary, shared beliefs. An equivalent text within social work does not exist, but as will be seen, the ideas put forward are very much relevant to social work. These include the 'five focal' virtues of compassion, discernment, integrity (personal and professional), trustworthiness and conscientiousness (see Figure 2.3). Beauchamp and Childress link these virtues to the moral principles of autonomy, beneficence, non-maleficence and justice. Each of these moral principles will be discussed below.

Figure 2.3 Five focal virtues as defined by Beauchamp and Childress (2009)

Autonomy comes from the Greek words '*autos*' (meaning 'self') and '*nomos*' meaning 'rule'. It originally referred to independent states or cities but has since come to refer to people. The central tenet of this principle is that, whenever possible, individuals should be treated as autonomous: independent and able to make their own decisions. Social workers are expected to 'practise as an autonomous professional, exercising their own professional judgment' as well as to be able 'to support service users and carers to control their lives and make informed choices about the services they receive' (HCPC 2012, Standards of Proficiency 4 and 9.4 respectively, p.8 and p.11).

This leads to the principle of beneficence – the obligation 'to do good'. Where a service user lacks capacity, or is not able to make autonomous decisions, social workers have an obligation to ensure that they can make 'informed decisions' (HCPC 2012, Standards of Proficiency 9.4, p.11) or in some situations, they may have to make informed decisions on their behalf, alongside carers, family, friends and other professionals. Many social workers initially entered the profession because they had a high motivation to meet this obligation. They wanted to help people.

The origins of the third principle, non-maleficence, are unclear, but the term has been linked to its Latin equivalent of *'maxim primum non nocere'*, which translates as 'above all, do no harm'. Unfortunately, harm can be done in many ways. There are straightforward mistakes (such as not following an organisational procedure appropriately), through action or inaction (e.g. not assessing the seriousness of a situation so that a service user then goes on to harm others), and through systemic failings (such as children who may drift for years in the care system). Social workers are accountable for their practice. But often the repercussions of their decisions do not become clear until years later, when they have moved on to other posts but service users are still caught up in 'the system'.

The fourth principle is justice. Beauchamp and Childress (2009, p.226) describe this as 'the fair and appropriate treatment in light of what is due or owed to persons'. The PCF (SWRB 2011) have placed a renewed emphasis on social workers' responsibilities in this area under the capability of 'rights, justice and economic well being'. Spicker (cited in Banks 2006) refers to justice as equality, and distinguishes between equal treatment, equal opportunity and equality of result. Banks (2006) argues that social workers should be concerned about promoting all three types. Within an offending context, there are different types of justice. Banks and Gallagher (2009) distinguish between legal, distributive, retributive, restorative and transformative justice.

If a primary aim of many practitioners is to enter the profession to help others, a significant number also see themselves as challenging injustice and inequality, especially for service users who may not be able to do this for themselves. A related principle to those above is that of paternalism. Beauchamp and Childress (2009, p.226) refer to this as 'the intentional over riding of one person's preferences or actions by another' – whether that is justified or not. At times, social workers are put in a position where they limit the autonomy and self-determination of service users. Sometimes they do this because they believe they are acting benevolently, 'for the good', at other times it may be to avoid harm or offer some kind of justice. The process of ethical decision making will be explored further in Chapter 4.

Kitchener (cited in Haverkamp and Daniluk 1993) adds two further principles – fidelity and self-interest. Fidelity is about honesty – will a professional do what they say they will do? Will duties be performed in an honest and trustworthy fashion? It may seem strange to cite 'self-interest' as an ethical principle, especially as ethics is largely founded on the basis that moral obligations override self-interest. However, this principle becomes important in situations where social workers are obliged to carry out duties that do not fit in with their personal beliefs, or may work in situations where poor practice is rife. All six principles will be explored further in Chapter 4.

It can be seen from the above discussion how readily the Beauchamp and Childress (2009) principles can be applied to social work. However, like virtue ethics and the ethics of care, they do not offer a framework of what to do in specific situations, but do provide some useful concepts to help think about ethical issues in practice.

Having discussed the main ethical theories, it may be helpful to review their relevance to social work. Whilst the values matrix (Figure 1.1) locates the place of values within social work, the matrix of ethical theories (see Figure 2.4) shows each of the ethical theories and the types of questions or issues that are related to them in social work. The principles approach is located in the centre of the matrix, as the principles span across the different theories. Both of the matrices will be referred to throughout the rest of the book.

So far this chapter has focused on different ethical theories and their relevance to social work. For some, it may seem a significant omission to discuss ethics and, in a sense, morality without any reference at all to religion or spirituality. This will be explored next.

Deontology	Virtue ethics
What are my professional duties? How am I balancing respect for service users (and their wishes) with my duties?	What needs to change/be different for this service user to have a positive outcome? What aspects of my practice are working well and what needs further development?
Principles	
Utilitarianism	Ethics of care
How can I meet this service user's needs within the resources that I have access to? How can I balance the needs of this service user with the needs of others – within the family or within my organisation?	What is the quality of the relationship between myself and the service user? What is the quality of the relationship between the service user, their family and wider support networks?

Figure 2.4 The matrix of ethical theories

The place of religion and spirituality within ethical theory

It was noted at the beginning of the chapter that early philosophers were keen that ethical theories would be based on reason alone and not be connected to science or religion. This position supports current social work in the western world, which adopts a secular position. This was not always the case. Social work in the UK originated with religious based charitable organisations, some like Barnardos and Action for Children (which started out as National Children's Home) continue their work today (Beckett and Maynard 2009).

This secularised approach in social work is one way of separating a practitioner's cultural and personal value base from their legal and professional obligations. It recognises that religions can be sources of oppression, as well as places of spirituality. However, there is a danger that this has led to workers having a lack of spiritual literacy

(Holloway and Moss 2010). For example, if religion is seen as off limits, this aspect of service users' lives is then ignored.

Social workers provide specialist services, often at a point of crisis. This means that they have a chronic exposure to the aspects of peoples' lives that are functioning least well. Whatever the service user group, religion or spirituality can be seen to have a potent – often debilitating – influence. For example, service users with serious mental ill health can often have paranoid thoughts that are religiously based. Mental health social workers (especially approved mental health practitioners) may need to work hard to clarify if a service user is expressing concerns that are legitimately connected to their spirituality, or if the thoughts are part of their illness, connected to their psychosis. Understanding the place of religion and spirituality can become crucial in any assessment. A chilling example of this not happening is the death of Victoria Climbié, whose carers were convinced that a demon possessed her. This ultimately contributed to their mistreatment of her (Laming 2003). Victoria was taken to a number of African churches where her aunt and aunt's boyfriend had sought advice around the best way of exorcising her.

Having exposure to cases such as these, as well as their secular training, can inadvertently result in social workers not being able to see the positive aspects of one's spirituality. Religion can be a source of strength and support. The formal practice of it can connect people to a whole community or at least to a system of support, which could provide sustenance and a source of emotional resilience.

For the practitioner, working in a secular way can dislocate one's sense of spirituality (however that is defined by them), from one's practice. One example is the burnt out social worker who entered the profession feeling that it was her 'calling', the need to help others, but over the years has learned to define her role in terms of her duties and so performs them in a more and more unthinking, autonomous manner.

Whether you define yourself according to a religion, or as an atheist, an agnostic or a theist, you will still need to be aware of your own sense of morality and how this affects your assessment of service users and their sense of morality.

Thompson (2010, p.152) looked at how religion and morality are related and offers three possibilities:

1. Autonomy — morality is completely separated from religion. Any similarities are purely coincidental.

2. Heteronomy — morality is dependent and based on religious beliefs or values.

3. Theonomy — morality and religion both originate from God.

Points to consider

- How do you define your spirituality?

- Where does it originate from? (e.g. is it from your family of origin, religion, culture, your profession, or your own sense of 'morality' that is separate from these factors?)

- How do you work with religion and spirituality?

This chapter has so far looked at different ethical theories that have influenced western social work, and at the place of religion and spirituality. Table 2.1 provides a summary of the main theories and some of their key points.

Some of the theories may have 'spoken' to you, or may have seemed more relevant than others. They have certainly stood the test of time. The earliest theories, like Aristotle's, have taken on almost mythical qualities. In this vein, this chapter will end with a story, a fairy story (and of course an exercise). Social workers are adept at taking in lots of information, and at hearing other peoples' stories. So this is an exercise to see how much information you can remember.

Table 2.1 A summary of ethical theories and their key points

Theory	Name of theorist	Key points
Virtue ethics	Aristotle	It is important to acquire good habits by optimising the development of the 12 key moral virtues.
		What are the traits of a 'good' social worker'?
Deontology	Kant	Moral laws (such as lying) are universalisable.
		Treat everyone with respect in their own right.
		Treat others as you would wish to be treated.
Utilitarianism	Bentham, Mill	The usefulness of an act depends on the principle of 'utility', of how much happiness it is likely to bring to the greatest number of people.
		'Harm principle' – that we can all do whatever we like as long as our actions do not harm others or ourselves.
The ethics of care	Gilligan	The vulnerable in society need care. It is usually women who provide this, and in doing so, need to focus on the emotional response, the quality of the relationship that is developed in providing that care.
Principles approach	Beauchamp and Childress	The importance of working to the principles of beneficence, non-maleficence, autonomy and justice (also the principles of fidelity and self-interest).
Religion/ spirituality		What impact do my or the service user's religious or spiritual beliefs have on this situation?
		In my view, what is the morally right thing to do, in this situation? How does this fit in with my professional duties?

In this fairy tale, a king is visited by the ghosts of three wise men.

A Fairy Tale: The Ghosts of the Three Wise Men

Long, long ago, there was once a king who ruled a prosperous and thriving nation. Over the years, he worked hard to make links with his neighbours, to ensure the long-standing peace of his nation. Yet he remained dissatisfied. He wanted answers to some of the bigger questions. The king wanted to safeguard the long-standing happiness and well being of every subject.

The ghosts of three wise men heard of this and came to visit him, one by one.

The first ghost was Immanuel Kant (1724–1804). He was born in Konigsberg, a small village in Prussia. During his life, Kant's fame had spread widely, despite him never venturing more than ten miles beyond the village of his birth. So the king felt excited at this arrival.

Kant declared that his approach (deontology) studied the science of duty (*deon* = duty, *logos* = science). The king was impressed. After all, his whole life was taken up with a supreme sense of duty for his subjects. Now here was a man who acknowledged the place of duty for each and every member of society.

'Why have I not considered this before?' He pondered. 'If I have a duty towards my subjects, surely, they also have a duty towards me, and to each other? Please – tell me more.'

Kant had worked hard to uncover certain 'universal truths'. He called these 'categorical imperatives'. He had made many 'formulations' but spelt the following out to the king:

'1. Act in such a way as your actions can and ought to be "universalisable".

2. Treat people as ends in themselves and never solely as a means to an end.

3. Act in such a way as you would have others act towards you.'

It took some time for the king to understand these. 'Am I right in thinking that your main focus is a supreme respect for each human being?'

'That is most eloquently put, your Majesty.'

'So, if we all have certain moral duties, they are in the way we treat and behave towards each other?'

'Quite so.'

Although the king was surrounded by privilege, he was not naive.

'I wonder what happens when some of these duties conflict with each other? The other day, for example, my younger brother (Prince Tobias) arrived, having fled some far away land after having broken a minor law there. Some warriors came looking for him. It was all rather embarrassing. I was torn between my duty to speak the truth and my duty to protect a loved one. Tell me, what do you say of such situations?'

'Your Majesty, I say, although the world may perish, let justice be done! What would happen if everyone lied? Society could not function – a man's word would have no value at all. No, a lie is never justified.'

The king was rather unhappy at this response. The next ghost to visit him was Aristotle (384–322 BCE). Aristotle was used to offering advice to royalty. He had regularly met with King Philip II and had taught his son, Alexander the Great.

'Your Highness,' he began, 'The key is for each and every member of society to live a life of "*eudaimonia*" – that is a good and virtuous life.'

'That sounds most honourable,' said the king. 'Tell me more.'

'Well, your Majesty, to have the potential of being happy, one must acquire good moral habits – you know, develop a good character, full of virtuous habits. I call my studies of this "virtue ethics".'

'Does this mean drawing up long lists of virtues that we must then work hard to aspire to?' The king did not like making lists. It felt rather onerous. 'What happens if, for whatever reason, we are unable to reach the dizzying heights of such perfection? I admit, I have a tendency towards impatience – does that mean I am unfit to be a king?'

Aristotle smiled, 'A virtuous person does what a virtuous person would do, your Majesty. This means giving the best jobs to the people best able to do them.'

The king had heard enough and told Aristotle he was free to go. He was feeling a little irked and was trying to recover his equanimity when he was told that the third and final ghost (Jeremy Bentham, 1748–1832) had arrived, and was escorted by a student of his (John Stuart Mill, 1806–1873).

With great ceremony, a wooden cabinet was wheeled into the Royal Court followed by an Englishman, in nineteenth-century attire, who was introduced as John Stuart Mill.

The king looked around, 'Yes, I understand you have a student with you?'

'Your Majesty, I *am* the student,' replied the man, bowing deeply. 'Please allow me the privilege of presenting the man with whom I studied: Mr Jeremy Bentham.' Mr Mill swung open doors of the wooden cabinet to reveal what looked like an embalmed corpse.

'Your Mr Bentham seems rather unwell.' The king tried not to look too bewildered.

'Oh, he is quite dead and has been since…'

'I should think so! His head looks like it is made of wax!' The king's impatience was getting the better of him.

'I am afraid the embalmer rather messed up his head, so we've had to improvise, your Majesty. It was Mr Bentham's wish that he be embalmed so that he could retain a permanent influence on the students of University College London, the institution he contributed in founding. This cabinet is usually located there. Your Majesty, this may seem eccentric, but, if your bear with me, I can assure you our philosophy is sound.'

'And that is?'

'Utilitarianism – the greatest happiness for the greatest number of people.'

'Well, that is certainly what I am seeking – for the happiness of my subjects. But how do you define happiness? Is it in terms of financial security? Is it health and well being? Is it ensuring that I have no unemployment in my kingdom? What are the main principles of your approach?'

'Ah, in actual fact,' said Mr Mill, 'We don't have any principles as such. That is because the right action, in any given situation is the action that will produce the most happiness for the greatest number of people. If I may be as bold as to go further – I could not help overhearing the earlier reference about the plight of your brother, Prince Tobias...'

'Yes – what do you suggest I do?' The king was beginning to lose hope of getting a sensible answer.

'Ahem – well, your Majesty, with all due respect, it seems a huge step you appear to be taking – to sacrifice the peace and happiness of your entire nation, for the well being of one person!'

This was too much. The king dismissed the embalmed Mr Bentham and Mr Mill and ordered tea to be served in his chambers. He was coming down with one of his headaches.

As he retired, his daughter, Princess Sophia joined him.

'Father, I have heard of your visitors this morning,' she smiled.

'I do not wish to talk of them at present,' sighed the king.

'Of course, father. Perhaps when you are feeling better, we can ask some wise women to visit and speak with you.'

'Wise women, you say? How interesting. You'll be telling me they are feminists next.'

'Indeed, father. Your wise men seem to have forgotten the importance of relationships, of the responsibility we have for those in our care, and the need to do whatever it takes to further the best interests of the vulnerable.'

'I suppose it is your friend, Carol Gilligan, to whom you are referring?'

'Yes, father. And others – such as Nel Noddings. Their work around the "ethics of care" is most thought provoking. Women do form nearly half of your subjects, so it is important that you hear about their experiences and needs.'

'Yes, dear. You must invite them over for tea one day...' The king was about to retire. Princess Sophia spoke quickly.

'Father, I have already consulted with them about Uncle Tobias and his plight. Of course, we have a duty of care to him. And if our country were to go to war, we would have a huge duty of care to the women and children left behind, and to any wounded soldiers on their return. This situation cannot persist. Perhaps we could send a generous gift and apology to our neighbours, as a peace offering, along with a donation to a charity of their choice?'

'My dear, you speak wise words for one so young.' He gave his daughter's hand a gentle squeeze. 'It shall be done. Please thank your friends and ask them to tea next week.'

With that, the exhausted king retired to his chambers for a well-deserved rest.

Table 2.2 highlights some of the concepts from the different theories and what their relevance is to social work. The left hand column (naming the ethical theory) has been left blank for you to complete. (The answers are at the bottom of this page.)

Can you identify which ethical approach describes the following concepts?

- Deontology
- Utilitarianism
- Virtue ethics
- Ethics of care

Conclusion

This chapter has introduced the main ethical theories. It has given an overview of the theory followed by a discussion of its relevance to social work. The coming chapters will build on this by discussing ethical issues within the framework of the matrix of ethical theories.

The need for practitioners to develop a sense of spiritual literacy has been discussed. This tends to go against the secular training received by most social workers but offers an opportunity for them to rethink their own practice within the framework of their own spirituality – however that is defined by them.

Once again, the links are made between personal values and the impact it has on practice. This is a theme that will be further developed in the next chapter.

Answers to Table 2.2 Exercise
1: Deontology; 2: Utilitarianism; 3: Ethics of care; 4: Virtue ethics; 5: Ethics of care; 6: Virtue ethics; 7: Deontology; 8: Utilitarianism

Table 2.2 Exercise: Can you identify the correct ethical theory?

Ethical theory	Concepts	Relevance to social work
1 Deontology	'Treat people as ends in themselves and never solely as a means to an end'	The basic concept of human dignity: all humans have worth
2	'Harm principle': Individuals should be free to act as they wish, as long as they do not harm others	Safeguarding vulnerable people against harm
3	Emphasises the interdependence of human relationships	Highlights the invisible role of carers
4	Identifying the right traits for each job	Competence in professional practice
5	The vulnerable need extra consideration	Balancing the conflicting rights and needs of different people in any given situation
6	Emphasis on moral excellence	Continuing professional development
7	'Act in such a way as you would have others act towards you'	Respect for others
8	Equal rights to all: abolish slavery, legalise homosexuality and allow women to vote	Emphasis on justice and equality; recognition of the value of diverse communities

CHAPTER 3

Changing Values in Professional Life

Key messages

- There are different stages of professional development and values can change over time.

- Newly qualified social workers tend to split personal values from professional ones, whilst more experienced practitioners are in danger of reverting to stereotypical judgements about service users.

- Losing the link between one's values and practice contributes to poor practice and leads to burn out.

Case study

As a child, Heddy had been a carer for her disabled mother. A concerned teacher had taken her under her wing and eventually a charity working with young carers provided much-needed support. These formative experiences were key in Heddy's decision to become a social worker.

She enjoyed her training and had been excited about starting out in her chosen career. She had wanted, quite passionately, to be able to help others in the way that she had been helped.

Now, two and half years later, she felt exhausted – physically and emotionally. Most of the service users she worked with did not value or want her help. Some were downright abusive. Her caseload was unmanageable. Heddy was aware that she had built a hard shell around herself and learned to separate herself from her work. She had stopped caring. In many ways she was working mechanically, having cut herself off from the very values she held dear. She realised she was at risk of burn out.

Introduction

This chapter builds on the value matrix presented in Chapter 1, focusing on its centre: values. It explores how values can change in professional life. Social work places great emphasis on professional values. In Heddy's case (above), as in so many others, personal values can influence the decision to come into the profession. It is then the expectation that professional values will be accepted and adopted. For some, there will be little disparity between the two. For others, there is a greater disparity. There may be clashes between personal and professional values. Learning to be aware of these clashes and taking appropriate action, is a vital ingredient in keeping practitioners effective. When practitioners work mechanically, cutting themselves off from their values, they are more likely to practise dangerously and become burnt out.

To begin with in this chapter, there will be an exploration of how social work skills develop over time and the possible impact this can have on changing professional values. There will then be an exploration of the different stages of becoming a professional. For some practitioners, this means that their values also evolve over time. The link between personal and professional values is explored. It is suggested that a lack of attention to this contributes towards ineffective practice and the danger of becoming burnt out. Some tools are presented to enable reflection in this area: how to develop more awareness of your 'self' and strategies that can be used to better manage or 'contain' your emotions at work, as well as suggestions to develop 'wellness' and prevent burn out.

The evolving professional

Qualifying in social work is experienced as a huge achievement, often one involving not only hard work, but many personal sacrifices. It can be a time of anticipation, especially if students have had positive learning experiences on placement. They may want to build on the skills they have gained and may be looking forward to the challenge, responsibility and greater financial reward attached to being a qualified social worker. There will inevitably be trepidation, anxiety, a concern about being 'good enough', about being able to manage caseloads and stress, or whether they will have a manager who will give them the support needed to continue developing. Some will have a clear idea of their career pathway, others will need to take things one step at a time.

Points to consider

- What were your hopes, aspirations, fears and anxieties when you qualified?

- Consider your first position as a newly qualified worker. Why did you apply for and accept that post?

- Complete the questionnaire in Table 3.1 by ticking all of the rows that apply to you, to see what (if anything) has changed since you qualified.

You may find your values have not essentially changed. Or there may be some significant shifts. Sometimes life changes may bring a clash of values between your personal and professional lives, for example, having a child of your own whilst working within the area of child protection can raise potent feelings. Workers may need to reassess if they can continue working within that area, or if they need to move to another team. Although there may be a range of reasons for this (e.g. need for greater work–life balance, need to meet parenting responsibilities, feeling that being a parent has somehow made them more sensitive to the emotional impact of working daily with child abuse), the issue is often one of realigning personal and professional values.

Most practitioners will clearly remember their first years in practice. If they were part of a supportive team, often the friendships created within them last many years. In recent times, there has been an increasing recognition of the vital role played in the first year or so of practice in enabling practitioners to step up from being a newly qualified social worker, to being a proficient practitioner. This has lead to the Assessed and Supported Year in Employment (SWRB 2010). What is not so commonly explored is how social workers and their practice evolve over a longer period of time. This is what will be looked at next.

Table 3.1 Exercise: Why did you become a social worker? Why do you remain a social worker?

Reason for entering social work	Reason for remaining in social work	Value/motivator
		Promotion: having the opportunity to excel in your job and be promoted
		Money: earning a decent salary; having the opportunity to earn money through over time and outside work, if necessary
		Working conditions: your day to day work environment
		Hours: working hours to suit your needs and interests
		Helping clients: enabling others to improve the quality of their lives
		Relationships: working as a team; working well with others, developing friendships with colleagues
		Learning: enjoying learning new skills and knowledge, both outside and within the context of work
		Recognition: having your skills and knowledge recognised and appreciated; being taken seriously and given credit for a job well done
		Security: ensuring you have a job which does not carry the threat of redundancy
		Time: having time to pursue interests outside work
		Stress-free work: work which is free of pressure, anxiety and deadlines
		Diversity: a job which offers the chance to do different kinds of work, and develop new skills and work in different ways

cont.

Table 3.1 Exercise: Why did you become a social worker? Why do you remain a social worker? *cont.*

Reason for entering social work	Reason for remaining in social work	Value/motivator
		Freedom: having the freedom to make decisions to have maximum control over your day to day work
		Admiration: carrying out work which others will admire you for
		Practitioners: practising your profession with clients and others
		Manager: managing and organising the work of others; developing policies and implementing procedures
		Other: values which are important to you

Source: Reprinted with kind permission from Alix Walton, Royal Holloway, University of London; adapted from Hull and Redfern (1996)

1. Developing professional competence

There is limited research on how social work values impact on professional development and how they may or may not change over time. Dreyfus and Dreyfus (1986), in their five-stage model, looked at how professionals developed over time. They focused on the types of skills and knowledge that are gained at different levels of professional development. They outlined five stages of development: novice, advanced beginner, competent worker, proficient worker and expert.

They found that novices were more likely to have prescribed ways of thinking and were more likely to adhere rigidly to rules, whereas experts tended to work much more intuitively with a more flexible and dynamic grasp of regulations. It makes sense that a newly qualified practitioner would be careful to ensure that they followed the correct procedures and worked within their agency's policies. As they developed their skills and greater experience, they would have the confidence to work more intuitively and flexibly.

Fook, Ryan and Hawkins (2000) built on this work by interviewing students before they embarked on social work training, following them throughout their social work course and then up to three years after they qualified. As their extensive findings are particularly relevant to this chapter, it draws heavily on their research.

The findings were similar to Dreyfus and Dreyfus (1986) in many respects but the five-stage model of professional development was expanded into a seven-stage model:

1. pre-student

2. beginner (starting social work training)

3. advanced beginner (completing social work training)

4. competent

5. proficient

6. experienced

7. expert.

Fook *et al.*'s (2000) findings show that people entering social work training started off with general ideas about wanting to help people. They started training by using their own personal experience as a compass to make sense of the learning process. Increasingly, there was a shift towards developing specific skills (e.g. assessment skills). By the time they qualified, most students had a sense of themselves as a social worker and some confidence in their skills.

Newly qualified social workers started their careers by focusing on policies and procedures. They wanted to familiarise themselves with the organisation they worked in, to develop a working knowledge of appropriate legislation and to generally become adept at the roles they were expected to fulfil. They tended to have little use of theory to guide their practice but, instead, wanted to build on and consolidate their practice-based learning.

As they became more familiar with their roles and developed some degree of competence, they developed a more personal style of practice ('doing it your way' [p.100]); they became more aware of their role in the organisation and of the context in which the organisation operated. They were more able and confident in 'selling the profession to others' (p.184).

Over time, experienced practitioners built up a level of knowledge and experience that enabled them to 'juggle complexity' (p.182) and to work within a climate of uncertainty. Their assessments became holistic in nature. They developed their own theories.

It was interesting to note how a few practitioners become labelled as experts. They found that experience and time, in and of themselves, were not enough to guarantee that a practitioner would develop into an expert. In fact some workers acquired this status quite quickly after qualifying.

Experts had specific characteristics. They had a sound understanding of legislation, policy and procedures, as one would expect but, somehow, they practised in a way that was more than simply the sum of these skills. They worked flexibly and intuitively; constantly expanding their pool of knowledge and experience and using this to go on and develop their own theories about their work. Experts were 'critically reflective' (p.232). They worked in a holistic way, being mindful of the complex issues relating to the service users. They worked well with other professionals and their agencies. These practitioners became 'grounded yet transcendent' (p.183). Their feet were firmly rooted in good practice but their sense of themselves as a professional came not from the organisation they worked for; rather, they saw social work as their calling, not simply a job they had to do.

Points to consider

- How have your skills developed over time? (Consider your skills in building relationships with service users and professionals, your assessment skills, your ability to analyse and reflect on complex and uncertain situations.)

- How would you evaluate your skills? Where have you improved? What areas do you need to continue working on?

- How confident are you as a professional, in building a case and arguing for what you believe is in your client's best interest?

2. The link between personal and professional values

Another interesting facet of Fook *et al.*'s (2000) research is that it explored how professional values changed over time. Some of the findings will be discussed in detail here, and applications made to social workers' evolving values.

The researchers found that students starting social work training tended to have 'unformed and uninformed concern' (p.182); that is, they tended to have rather general and nebulous ideas around wanting to help people. Many students were not clear about what their personal values were, but the process of undergoing social work training helped to clarify this. By the time most students had completed their training, they tended to hide or submerge their personal values, in an attempt to gain objectivity and get the job done.

These newly qualified workers started off professional practice by being 'constrained conformists' (p.182), rarely making reference to their personal values. Somehow, these were pushed to one side, as an effort was made to work in a neutral, judgement-free way. There is a sense here of individuals being aware of some aspects of social work being in conflict with their personal world view, but that reconciling this with their duties was too difficult a task. It was simply easier to split off their personal and professional lives. For example, a worker could have strong feelings about working with a parent who misused drugs in front of their children. They might be scathingly judgemental of them, but learned to push these feelings aside, to work with them in a 'neutral' way.

Fook *et al.* (2000) found that within two to three years most practitioners had developed into either 'proficient' or 'competent' workers. Both were experienced and able to practise. There were, however, important differences between the two types of worker. 'Proficient' workers embraced the 'personal and the political' (p.182) in social work by consolidating their professional identity. Perhaps they did this by finding a way of enabling their personal and professional values to coexist alongside one another, or perhaps they did not feel there was a huge conflict between them in the first place. In any case, they were aware of their role within the agency and were confident in representing the profession positively.

'Competent' workers, on the other hand, had learned to 'get along in the system' (p.181) and to 'forget social work – get the job done!' (p.182). This phrase suggests that although the workers were competent, that some degree of cynicism had developed. The reasons for this were not explored. Some dissonance is implied here, between one's expectation about social work and what is experienced in reality; a giving in to something. Social work is full of contradictions. A profession that places so much emphasis on service users' rights, on the one hand, also carries immense powers of control on the other. Teams set up to provide essential services for vulnerable people still need to make tough decisions about the allocation of resources. So it is at least understandable that some practitioners should find that their personal beliefs and values about how services should be provided were not matched by the reality of the job.

After about three years in practice, the research team found that practitioners were able to work well with uncertainty and complexity and were adept at unpicking ethical issues. There was, however, also a surprising finding. It was that some very experienced workers were *more* likely (than less experienced workers):

(a) to make judgemental, stereotypical statements about service users. For example, a practitioner working with a young black man who had offended commented that it was pointless intervening as the young man's life was already mapped out.

(b) to sympathise with service users from a similar social location as themselves, whilst pathologising those that were very different, or other than themselves. (See example in (a) above.)

Fook *et al.* coined the term 'social distancing' (p.184) and used it to describe the process where a worker sees particular people or groups *other* than oneself. This could be seeing them as socially different, but it implies that they are seen as so different from oneself that there is inability to be able to empathise or relate to them. This was particularly found to be the case for men who were black, or of working class origin, and led to a reluctance from some practitioners to deal with them, especially if they tended to display angry, aggressive or violent behaviour.

The suggestion seems to be that once practitioners have mastered policies, procedures and organisational systems, once they are experienced in handling complexity and uncertainty, with these skills well within their comfort zones, somehow they lose sight of the impact of their personal judgements and assumptions about people. There is the potential in these situations for workers to develop dangerous working practices, or to become burnt out. Both of these issues will be explored later in this chapter.

How do 'expert' social workers' values change over time? Fook *et al.*'s (2000) research showed that they, too, no longer feel the need to submerge their personal values. Instead, they were able to move beyond their professional codes and work to a broader set of values. They remained critically self-reflective, often exceeding expectations of what would normally be expected in good practice.

Table 3.2 summarises social work professional development and maps the different values positions practitioners can have at different points in their career.

So far, this chapter has explored how social workers develop professional competency and how, in this process, their values may evolve. They are likely to begin their careers by separating their personal values from their professional values, as they learn the basic skills of their trade. There is the danger that, as they become more experienced, they will learn to distance themselves from service users and allow value judgements about service users to creep in to their practice.

It could be argued that these are, in some ways, coping strategies, defences against the pressure of casework; of working with service users who may have limited insight into their difficulties and much resistance to change. However, if such practices continue unchecked, they can cause significant harm to service users, in the way they are assessed and have decisions made about them. Social workers can also cause harm to themselves, with chronic stress and burn out.

As will be seen later in this chapter, preventing burn out is easier than recovering from it. Also, developing a greater awareness of one's 'self' and how to manage emotions become essential skills in the establishment of a long term career in social work. This will be explored next.

Table 3.2 The seven stages of professional development

Stage of development	Skills gained	Impact on personal values
'Pre-student'	General ideas about 'helping people'	General concern
'Beginner' – starting social work training	Reliance on own personal experience	Beginning to learn professional ethics and values
'Advanced beginner' – completed social work training	Have developed specific skills and confidence in their own practice	Have learned to hide personal values, concerned about adapting to 'professional values'
'Competent'	Concerned with 'doing the job' and performing appropriately	Acting as 'constrained conformists' whose focus is to 'forget social work – get the job done!'
'Proficient'	Have learned strategies to deal with professional and organisational conflict and worked out how they can 'make a difference'	Less conformist; able to embrace the 'personal and political' and consolidate their professional identity
'Experienced'	Can manage uncertainty, are aware of their own limitations, learn from their mistakes and can create their own theories	Able to separate out their personal values from the expectations of their employers; can learn to 'socially distance' themselves from service users, making judgemental comments about them
'Expert'	Can use their knowledge creatively, recognising multiple viewpoints. Adept at responding to change and uncertainty, generating a range of options	'Grounded yet transcendent': practice according to a broad value base and working 'beyond the call of duty'

Source: Adapted from Fook *et al.* (2000)

The 'self'

Case study

Heddy had been working in a 'Children in Need Team' for six months when she started working with Petra – a 15-year-old girl who was showing signs of psychosis.

Petra said she heard voices telling her to kill her parents. Petra's parents were convinced that she was trying to kill them, but showed signs of mental illness themselves. The family had set up complex rituals and procedures to protect each other from harm. These resulted in Petra being isolated for much of the time. She had not gone to school for six months.

After many phone calls and discussions, Heddy was able to set up a professionals' meeting involving a child psychiatrist from the local Child and Adolescent Mental Health Service (CAAMHS). She had high hopes of getting some specialist input but was dismayed to find that she could not understand much of what the psychiatrist was saying. She had not come across this kind of language before. Heddy was distressed when the psychiatrist said that she had been 'colluding' with the family and should have been 'challenging the family's behaviour'. Although Heddy understood that the only practical way forward was to build up a good working relationship with the psychiatrist, she was at a loss as to how to do this.

Heddy's position highlights what complex situations social workers have to deal with and how easy it is to feel overwhelmed, and in a no-win position. It also demonstrates how, in every encounter, workers need to consider the impact they are having on service users, other professionals and also what impact the work is having on them 'selves'.

This concept of the 'self' is much used in social work and has its origins in psychoanalytic and psychodynamic theory. In the social work (rather than therapeutic) context, it refers to the different elements that make up who we are. This may include, for example, one's 'personal self' or 'professional self'. Looking at one's professional identity, an individual worker could further break down different aspects of themselves, for example, the part of themselves that enjoys building relationships with service users, the part they have actively developed to be able to work with hostile and resistant service users, or to follow their manager's instructions, or to appear confident when working with a range of professionals.

Workers who are connected to all aspects of them 'selves' are more likely to be good practitioners. Newly qualified workers, or workers who have been qualified for a long time and have developed an easy familiarity with their duties are most at risk of cutting themselves off from different aspects of them 'selves'.

In the case of newly qualified social workers, they may be anxious about following organisational policy and procedures, and are more likely to disconnect their 'personal selves' from their 'professional selves', whilst very experienced workers may defend themselves against the emotional impact of their work by disconnecting from their 'professional selves' by mechanically following procedures.

As Harrison and Ruch (2008, p.44) point out, to be able to practise ethically and soundly from an appropriate value base, 'requires engagement with the whole self – personally professional self and the professionally personal self'.

Managing the 'self'

Case study *continued*

Heddy already felt overwhelmed with the case. She now felt inadequate and attacked.

She wanted to understand psychoanalytic terms and so turned to some books she had used during her social work training. She recollected that she had read about Freud and had found his ideas somewhat difficult to follow.

She had no idea how she would manage her anxiety or how she would be able to bring about any positive changes for Petra and her parents.

Every day social work is full of powerful feelings. It is understandable that Heddy should feel overwhelmed. How easy it would be for her to cut off from some of these feelings. For example, she could try to disconnect from the part of her 'self' that is feeling professionally inadequate by perhaps getting angry with the consultant psychiatrist. She knows that the psychiatrist is well known in her team for making controversial remarks and is sure that mentioning the incident to a couple of colleagues would incite a heated discussion. This in itself, while not being a useful way forward, might provide some consolation in that she would not feel quite so isolated.

A trusted colleague who could offer impartial advice may serve Heddy better, as would an honest dialogue with her manager. There are times, however, when emotions can feel too raw to be discussed in a constructive way. At such moments, it is worth finding some space in which one can think through, tease out the different issues (perhaps in the form of a mind map) and then try to clarify:

- What are the different strands of this situation?

- What are the different feelings/thoughts/concerns you have?

- Clarify the areas that need professional action. How can things move forward?

- What support do you need and where will you get it from?

Figure 3.1 shows how answering the above questions helped Heddy to clarify in her own mind what action she needed to take.

Points to consider

How do you manage your emotions at work? Think about formal and informal strategies you may use:

- with your line manager (how effectively do you use supervision?)

- with colleagues

- with friends or a mentor

- during counselling or some other form of 'therapeutic' activity (e.g. exercise, meditation or something more social).

| **Describe the situation** |
| I am feeling overwhelmed with the 'P' case. |

What are the different feelings/thoughts/concerns?
(List them as you think of them, no order of priority.)

- I am worried sick that 'P' will hurt herself or her parents.
- Is she really mentally ill?
- Or has her parents' mental illness impacted on her (they have told her that she wants to kill them so many times that she has come to believe it as true)?
- What if I get my assessment wrong? I can't cope with the pressure!
- Maybe Mum was right – perhaps I'm not cut out for this kind of work!
- I have no idea what the psychiatrist was saying in that meeting.
- I can't believe she thinks I have colluded with the family! I have worked really hard on this case and spent many nights awake as a result.
- I have a real block about Freud – I am sorry, but I can't accept that Oedipal complex stuff – it's just sick!
- My team manager smiled knowingly when the psychiatrist said I was colluding. Does she agree with her? Does that make me a bad social worker? Does she think I am a bad social worker?
- Will this affect my appraisal? Maybe they will start disciplinary proceedings against me!

Way forward: Professional action points	**What support do you need and where will you get it from?**
In supervision, discuss how meeting went, making sure I cover the following points:	
- I struggled to understand psychiatrist and don't know how to move forward with this.	- I need to learn some of this psychological language quickly. Will talk to Sue (team member) she has a lot of experience in this area.
- Check out what my manager's views are about me 'colluding' with the family.	- Maybe I will ask her out to lunch and check out her views on the 'colluding'.
- Make sure we have a clear plan about what I have to do and that I understand it.	- The stress factor is way out of control – I think I need to book some leave!

Figure 3.1 Heddy's completed checklist

Wilfred Bion (Harrison and Ruch 2008) was a psychoanalyst and devised the term 'containment' to describe what happens when someone with unmanageable feelings is helped to manage them. For Bion, this process involved the person being 'thought about' in a way that enabled them to feel 'held' and so be better able to manage their feelings. Over time, this could lead to them developing the capacity to be able to think about their distress, and make sense of it, rather than simply be distraught by it.

Social workers are often put in positions of having to 'contain' the unmanageable feelings of service users. This will be discussed in more detail in the next chapter. Many social workers claim that if it wasn't for the support of team members they could not do their work so effectively. 'Containing' managers, colleagues, teams and work settings provide support and sustenance. This will be discussed further in Chapter 5. Although the concept of 'containment' may seem very simple, it is an important one to understand and apply appropriately.

In the current scenario, Heddy manages to 'contain' her emotions by spending a few minutes thinking through and clarifying what the different issues are. She initially blurts everything out on paper but can then move to a more reflective position, usefully identifying what she needs to do to move forward. Developing such strategies is a vital buffer against the endemically high stress levels inherent in social work. Heddy realises that her stress levels are spiralling out of control and that she needs to book some leave. Being able to identify when everyday stress is becoming unmanageable and to take proactive measures to counter it is essential to prevent burn out. The next section explores this further.

Identifying stress and avoiding burn out

Points to consider

- How do you know your stress levels are spiralling out of control?

- Are there specific areas of your life that are more prone to stress than others?

- What do you do to buffer the effects of stress?

In their national survey, the Social Work Task Force (Baginsky *et al.* 2010) found that 19 per cent of social workers were considering leaving the profession. Heightened stress was cited as one of the main reasons for this. It could be argued that high levels of stress are part and parcel of social work. However, Bride (2007) found that social workers in direct practice are at risk of becoming traumatised by their ongoing work with disturbed service users. He called this 'secondary traumatic stress' (STS) and concluded that, 'Many social workers are likely to experience at least some symptoms of STS, and a significant minority may meet the diagnostic criteria for PTSD [post traumatic stress disorder]' (p.63).

Stress is very real and, if left unattended, will over time, lead to burn out (Cherniss 1995). Factors that cause stress can be separated out into 'environmental stressors' (such as the physical aspects of work, the nature of the role, the quality of working relationships with colleagues and having too much work to do in too little time) and 'individual or personal' stressors which tend to focus on the personal response to stress, such as how an individual may respond to a specific client, their work–life balance, or how they interpret previous life events.

Unsurprisingly, stress in the helping professions is particularly prevalent, leading to high levels of 'burn out'. This is described as 'a type of prolonged response to chronic emotional and interpersonal stressors on the job…[that includes] emotional exhaustion, depersonalization and reduced personal accomplishment' (Maslach and Goldberg 1998, p.64).

How close are you to burn out? You can find out by completing the questionnaire in Table 3.3, designed using findings from Cherniss (1995) about the causes of stress. Just tick the box that is closest to the statement that fits how you are feeling right now.

Table 3.3 Exercise: Checklist – How close are you to burn out?

Tick the box that is closest to how you are feeling.

1: I can relate strongly to statement 'A'. 2: I can generally relate to statement 'A'. 3: I can relate equally to both statements. 4: I can relate generally to statement 'B'. 5: I can relate strongly to statement 'B'.

(Leave blank if you cannot relate to either statement 'A' or 'B'.)

	'A' Statements	1	2	3	4	5	'B' Statements
1	I love my work and feel it makes a real difference to the lives of service users.						My days are filled with pointless bureaucracy that achieves little change.
2	No two days are the same. Every day is a new and interesting challenge.						I am exhausted and overwhelmed by the constant battles I have with services users, other professionals and my line manager.
3	It is easy for me to create opportunities to try out something new.						I am very much in my comfort zone and often find my role tedious and boring.
4	I enjoy getting involved in projects that help improve practice.						There is no point in me volunteering for any special tasks – I am not one of the 'chosen' ones.
5	I love the autonomy of my role.						The level of responsibility I have scares me.
6	I have learned how to present my cases well at formal meetings and am confident at getting a good outcome.						I get stressed out at formal meetings. They always ask some long-winded questions that leave me confused.

cont.

Table 3.3 Exercise: Checklist – How close are you to burn out? *cont.*

'A' Statements	1	2	3	4	5	'B' Statements
7 Over time, I have learned how to manage office politics.						The office politics does my head in! You will not believe what goes on here!
8 I am fortunate to have a supportive line manager who I trust and have confidence in.						My manager is useless. I have no confidence or trust in their judgement.
9 I have flexible work arrangements and ample training opportunities.						My working hours are scrutinised like a hawk. I have no time to attend training sessions.
10 My colleagues are fun to work with, offer thoughtful suggestions and will go out of their way to help me.						My colleagues are as stressed out and as busy as I am. We are like ships passing in the night.
11 I make sure I take time out for training and for myself.						I am always behind in my work and can never take time out for training. My annual leave was cancelled due to an inspection.
12 I have realistic expectations of myself and those I work with and can set achievable targets.						I have a casual (*or* perfectionist) attitude which results in work being given back to be redone (it taking ages) for me to complete a task.

13	I am clear about where I will be, career wise, in five years time, and am steadily working towards this.	I am not sure about my career in social work and dream of leaving it every day!
14	I am an organised and self-sufficient person.	I need to get organised. My colleagues are fed up of me asking them for favours.
15	Over time, I have developed confidence in my ability to do a good job.	I am not sure about what is expected of me, and if I am honest, I am not sure if I am up to the job.
16	I have an insight into my strengths, weaknesses and preferences around my work and can take these into account.	I try hard to please my manager, but it feels like whatever I do is wrong.
17	I have a good work–life balance.	I am walking a fine line between disciplinary proceedings at work and a divorce at home. My kids don't recognise me anymore!
18	I have learned to pick my battles – fighting losing battles is a waste of time and energy.	I have been in a prolonged dispute with my employers but am determined to see it through. They will not get away with this…

How did you do?

Completing the questionnaire should help you to identify the different factors (positive and negative) that are contributing to your current experience of working life.

> **Statements 1–4** focus on the nature of the work itself, including your attitude towards the work you do, and what you do to try to keep yourself motivated and enthusiastic. Changing posts after about two to three years has been shown to buffer the effects of stress, as has moving on to a more senior or specialist position. However, it is not always necessary to try to work your way up an organisation's hierarchy. Moving sideways, into a different team or service, can be just as stimulating.

> **Statements 5–10** focus on the level of autonomy and support you have in your current position. Unsurprisingly, research shows that workers need to feel they have some degree of autonomy over their work, whilst at the same time feeling that they are being sufficiently supported to carry out their role. What are the things that you need to focus on in this area?

> **Statements 11–18** focus on your personal qualities as a professional. Looking at how you have answered the questions should help you to identify the areas you need to work on or change in your life, to avoid burn out. There may be areas that you need to actively shift to prevent burn out, whatever job you are doing.

Corey and Corey (1989) found that workers who had started their careers with an idealistic value base were more prone to burn out. These ideals can become dulled and tarnished over time. They discuss the importance of 'learning the fine balance between idealism and realism' if 'you hope to survive as a helping professional' (p.273). One of the ways of doing this is to ensure that you have active strategies for 'wellness' in place. The next section offers some suggestions.

Strategies for 'wellness'

What contributes towards a good work–life balance for you?

Nicolson, Bayne and Owen's (2006) extensive research in the area of stress in the caring professions repeatedly points to two things that consistently enable workers to remain healthy and buffer the effects of stress. These are expressive writing and getting peer group support.

The literature around expressive writing has flourished in recent years. This presents social workers with a range of tools that can be used to aid personal development. These may particularly 'speak' to practitioners who enjoy writing. Those who do not, or who may feel that issues such as dyslexia get in the way of their ability to write freely, may want to explore other strategies. It is still worth trying some form of expressive writing, as in this form of writing, there is no pressure to adhere to correct grammar or punctuation. What is important is that you connect to your thoughts and feelings. You may prefer to use mind maps or pictures instead of words. Three different types of expressive writing will be discussed: keeping a journal, 'clearing writing' and 'dialoguing'.

1. Keeping a journal

Nicolson *et al.* (2006) cite the leading researcher in the field of stress and the caring professions: James Pannebaker. Pannebaker and his team worked with a group of first year undergraduate students, splitting them into two random groups.

Each group was asked to write for 20 minutes for three consecutive days. One group was asked to write about what they had done that day (focusing on facts and behaviour) whilst the other was asked to write about their 'deepest thoughts and feelings'. It was found that the latter group were much less likely to go to the health centre in the coming six months. These results have since been replicated many times and have been used to underline the importance of writing about thoughts and feelings (as opposed to facts and behaviour) for maintaining good health.

If you do keep a journal, simply describing the events of the day will not help as a buffer against stress. For that, you will need to also connect with your thoughts and feelings.

Points to consider

Ten reasons for keeping a therapeutic journal:

1. You can access your journal whenever you want to at no cost.

2. Your journal will never get bored with your words.

3. You can create your own therapeutic map.

4. You can begin to hear your own voice.

5. You can get to know yourself deeply.

6. You can become better organised and able to cope.

7. You can practise for difficult or stressful experiences.

8. You can begin to appear more substantial and solid in your journal.

9. You can put all the unbearable bits of yourself in your journal and find they are bearable after all.

10. You can repair the narrative of your life in your journal.

(Thompson 2011, adapted from Adams 1993, p.31)

The use of keeping a journal for personal and professional development is well known (e.g. Cameron 2002; Klassen 2004; Thompson 2011). Amongst these, a common theme that emerges is for individuals to set aside essential time to reconnect with and replenish themselves so that they are not running 'on empty'.

Cameron (2002) suggests a weekly time where you down tools to do something (on your own) that will nurture your spirit. It could be going to an art gallery, or going for a swim and sauna. Many social workers will recognise the difficulty they have prioritising their own needs. It may feel hard enough trying to grab 20 minutes to pop out for a sandwich at lunch time, much less to plan a whole evening or afternoon for yourself. But even 20 minutes window shopping at lunch time can completely change your mind set and energy levels, setting you up to face the afternoon.

2. Clearing writing

Clearing writing is just that – using the power of words to clear yourself at an emotional level. Klassen (2004) recommends doing this for just five minutes, a free flow of whatever thoughts are preoccupying you. 'Emptying' your mind in this way frees up mental and emotional space. This can be essential to get you through turbulent times.

The following is part of an extract of Heddy's clearing writing:

Case study

'Woke up this morning feeling horrible about work and dreading going in. I am worried about the constant headaches I keep getting. I must pay the electricity bill. Ooops! Forgotten Jeff's birthday present... I must pick something up – no time today, will get home too late... I am so fed up of feeling tired all the time! I am fed up of feeling tired all the time! I am not coping and can't see how I am ever going to get on top of my work...'

Clearing writing is a personal outpouring – writing out all the noise in one's head, literally emptying the mind as much as possible in the short time available. In this type of writing, it is acceptable to repeat the same thing over and over again – if that is what is going on in your head. This may continue for weeks or months but, eventually, there will be a shift.

3. Dialoguing

Having become familiar with clearing writing, it can be helpful to then build on this by (re)connecting with different aspects of yourself and 'dialoguing' with them. This is particularly important during stressful times, when workers are apt to be in 'fight or flight' mode and more likely to disconnect from their usual 'selves'.

Dialoguing is a way of connecting to different aspects of yourself, simply by 'speaking' to them (in writing) and recording the answers. Some writers suggest asking the question with your usual writing hand and answering by writing with the other hand. But this is not essential.

Points to consider

Journal dialogues can help you to:

- make decisions
- look at unfinished business
- change or modify behaviour
- gain clarity and understanding
- overcome writing blocks
- come to terms with difficult decisions
- improve relationships and communication.

(Thompson 2011, p.131)

The following case study is an example of 'dialoguing', of Heddy connecting with and exploring some of her feelings around the psychiatrist's comments around her 'colluding' with Petra and her family instead of challenging their behaviour.

Case study

Me: I am so angry with Dr X. She is…!!!

Question: OK – why are you so angry with her?

Me: How dare she come in, when I have been working with the family for months, trying to get some agency – any agency to get involved – no one is interested. It is very easy for other professionals to criticise my work but they don't want to get involved themselves.

Question: Yes, but why are you angry with Dr X and her comments, in particular?

Me: She made me feel worthless. Utterly useless. Like I am a rubbish social worker!

Question: Are you a 'rubbish social worker'?

Me: I am not perfect. But I know I am not rubbish.

Question: So why did her comments press your buttons?

Me: It makes me angry — I work with the family for months and she rolls in and makes a 'diagnosis' in one meeting! I was angry because I couldn't get Petra to talk to me like she spoke to her. I am angry because she saw things that I didn't. I am angry because I came in to social work to make a difference, to work with vulnerable people. All I do is paperwork! I never have the chance to do any decent direct work. It is making me feel really de-skilled in that area. To be truthful, I don't know if I can do it at all.

In 'dialoguing' with herself in this way, Heddy is better able to understand her feelings and to name the different causes of them. She reconnects with the values that brought her in to social work and realises that part of her frustration in the current situation is about not being able to do the kind of work she would like to do (more direct work with young people). She can then discuss the possibilities of doing more direct work with her line manager. In other situations, the answer may not be so straightforward. However, 'dialoguing' has been shown to connect people to their 'inner wisdom' (Cameron 2002; Thompson 2011). Try it.

An important note: it is vital to do this work with compassion for yourself, so avoid getting into an abusive or self-attacking dialogue. Don't let it be another means of keeping you in a negative space.

Creating a peer support group

You may be fortunate enough to have access to strong and positive peer support from your work colleagues — informally through your team, or through relationships you have developed over time. If you don't, you may consider being proactive and setting up your own peer support group. Such groups can provide an important sense of belonging, as well as emotional support and validating one's professional practice. However, they can also be arenas where insensitive feedback can further undermine confidence and increase guilt at a poor intervention.

The following suggestions for running a successful group are amended from Nicolson *et al.* (2006, p.88):

- For each member of the group to have equal time.

- To agree ground rules.

- To agree boundaries around the work (e.g. that no discussion of any aspect of the group (process or content) happens outside the group).

- The person speaking to ask for the kind of support they would like (e.g. for people to listen, empathise, challenge, sharing factual information, advice, encouragement, constructive feedback).

- For periodic reviews to take place: What is working well? What could work better?

- For members to be aware of 'games' being played (such as 'ain't it awful', in which the group reinforce each other's sense of gloom and powerlessness; the three roles of victim, persecutor and rescuer in the Drama Triangle; see Chapter 5 for more details of this).

- For members to notice and challenge any interfering beliefs about asking for or accepting support. (Examples of interfering beliefs are: I don't have time; it's not fair on other people; I'm not worth it; it shows I can't cope; other people aren't interested; other people don't care; I can cope on my own; it may make me vulnerable.)

Other strategies for well being

Figure 3.2 illustrates the five essential aspects needed to ensure well being. Research into stress has repeatedly shown how a healthy, well balanced diet and regular exercise act as protective factors against stress and other types of disease. Even a moderate amount of regular exercise can act as a buffer (Gerber *et al.* 2010). However, these factors need to be balanced out with a good support network (Nahum-Shani and Bamberger 2011), some kind of connection with one's spirituality (whether that is a belief in God, or a higher power, or some kind of spiritually uplifting activity, such as listening to music or practising yoga). Finally, it has been shown that people living according to their values are more likely to be happier and live longer, compared to people who do not 'walk their talk' (Robbin 2006).

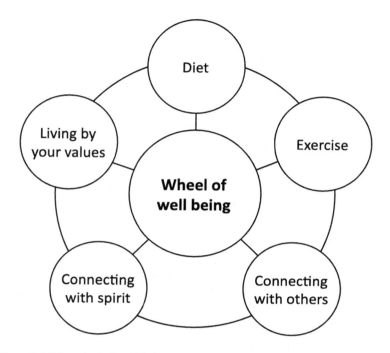

Figure 3.2 The wheel of well being

Points to consider

Here are some examples of buffers against stress:

- Listening regularly to music – especially soothing music, such as classical or meditative music. Bach, Mozart or the Italian composers were found to be especially effective in reducing stress (Lai and Li 2011; Trappe 2010).

- Yoga has been shown to have positive effects – sometimes these effects can be seen in less than a week (Narasimhan, Nagarathna and Nagendra 2011).

- People of faith, who regularly pray and attend church, were found to cope better with severe financial hardship than 'non-believers' (Bradshaw and Ellison 2010).

- Regular practice of autogenic training (a type of mind-body therapy that creates a deep sense of relaxation) was found to reduce hypertension (high blood pressure) and also provide greater control over IBS (irritable bowel syndrome) (Aivazyan 1988; Shinozaki *et al.* 2010).

If you are not sure how well your life style fits in with the above findings, an easy way of checking is by using the 'life expectancy calculator' (Perls 2012). You may also wish to check out the additional resources listed below.

Conclusion

This chapter has discussed practitioners' relationship between their personal and professional values. In the early years of practice there is a tendency to split off from one's values and focus on the 'professional task'. As more experience is gained, there is the danger of stereotypical judgements creeping into practice. Good supervision and reflective practice are protective factors in ensuring professional practice does not become dangerous and remains at a high standard.

Tools for developing a more explicit relationship with one's 'self' and also for assessing risk of and preventing burn out have been shared.

This chapter has focused on the central aspect of the values matrix (Figure 1.1), on values. How workers make sense of their changing values will depend on their ability to reflect on their experiences as a professional and to continue to align and realign their personal and professional values in an ongoing way. This may mean changing roles or jobs, or seeking out further professional training as a way of getting space to reflect and evaluate their practice, to update themselves on current research in a specific area and to generally support their continuing professional development.

Further reading and resources

Autogenic training: to find out more see www.autogenic-therapy.org.uk, accessed 17 August 2012.

Klassen, J. (2004) *Tools of Transformation: Write Your Way To New Worlds of Possibility.* West Conshohocken, PA: Infinity Publishing.

Mind offers a lot of resources on managing stress on their website, including the Mind Guide to Managing Stress, available at www.mind.org.uk/help/medical_and_alternative_care/mind_troubleshooters_stress, accessed 16 October 2012.

Perls (2012) provides a 'Life Expectancy Calculator' at www.livingto100.com, accessed 17 August 2012.

Thompson, K. (2011) *Therapeutic Journal Writing: An Introduction for Professionals.* London: Jessica Kingsley Publishers.

CHAPTER 4
Ethical Issues in Direct Work

Key messages

- Forming and maintaining appropriate boundaries in one's relationships with service users forms the bedrock from which all other work develops. Inappropriate professional relationships is the single most cited reason for social workers undergoing suitability proceedings.

- Power is multi-faceted and can switch quickly from being empowering, co-operative or protective to being oppressive, or collusive.

- In making ethical decisions practitioners need to distinguish between their personal values, their legal obligations, their responsibility to employers and their role in the organisation.

Introduction

On the one hand, I was committed to challenging oppression and, on the other, I had no choice but to oppress. At a basic level, how could I balance the conflicting rights of the disabled person and their carer? If I supported one, was it not inevitable that I would oppress the other?

(Gardener 2008, p.38)

Doing direct work with service users and wanting to make a difference to their lives is the main reason for people coming into social work (Baginsky *et al.* 2010). It also the most likely area in which ethical issues emerge. This chapter explores the three fundamental aspects of direct work: the setting of appropriate professional boundaries, the use of power and decision making. Social workers make assessments and decisions about service users in almost every encounter they have with them. There will be times when they have made a decision without even being aware that they have resolved an ethical issue. The principles approach is used in this chapter to clarify the ethical issues in a specific scenario from good practice.

To service users, the social worker is the face of the organisation they are representing. Social workers are the go-between, linking the service user to the resources available within the agency. 'Don't shoot the messenger' may be an apt saying in this context. There may be times when the social worker feels caught between the needs of the vulnerable people they work with and the needs of their organisation. For example, a social worker may feel that specialist residential care is needed, only to be told that this is not a viable option and that their assessment needs to be amended in line with available resources. Chapter 6 explores some of these organisational challenges in more detail. This chapter, and the following one, explore the dilemmas practitioners face in their everyday work with service users.

One of the most fundamental dilemmas faced in direct work with clients is where to draw the line between what is personal and what is professional. So this chapter starts by exploring boundaries, including service user perspectives of the helping relationship. This leads to a discussion about the use of power in working with service users and the ethical dilemmas that can arise from this.

Boundaries

The nature of the professional helping relationship necessitates one person helping the other in a particular sort of way. However, unlike family and friends, professionals are not helped in return. This gives professionals specific obligations to the people they help. Treating them with respect and dignity is one such obligation. Another is the obligation to 'uphold the intention of the relationship' (Mitchell 2011, p.155), in essence to keep appropriate, professional boundaries.

In their report on the review of social work professional conduct hearings, the General Social Care Council (GSCC 2008) found that over 40 per cent of all cases related to the crossing of professional boundaries and inappropriate relationships with service users. Moreover, the pattern tended to be not one of one-off transgressions, but of multiple and related transgressions that breached the trust and confidence of vulnerable service users and of the general public.

Ahmed (2011) gives the example of a social worker who sexually assaulted a teenager in his care. This may seem an extreme example and, fortunately, a rare one. For most social workers the issues around boundaries will be more subtle and perhaps more complex. How much personal information is it OK to disclose to service users? Under what circumstances (if any) is it OK to accept gifts?

Doel *et al.* (2010) found that practitioners base decisions regarding professional boundary violations on whether the behaviour would have a detrimental impact on public confidence in the profession ('consequentialist' or utilitarian factors) or on how specific behaviour was an indicator of a worker lacking professional integrity ('deontological' factors). They also found that personal moral codes were more likely to influence workers' actions than professional codes or organisational policies.

They make the important point that crossing professional boundaries can sometimes be a positive thing – such as workers 'going the extra mile' for clients or being brave enough to 'enter the shadows' of boundaries to ensure that the rights of service users are upheld. The term 'shadows' implies that there is no right or wrong answer to a specific behaviour; that a decision may depend on the context of a situation, or a range of other factors – such as confidentiality, self-disclosure, the nature of the relationship, and the time, place and context for a specific activity. Figure 4.1 shows these diagrammatically. Doel *et al.* suggest that 'the best way to help professionals avoid transgressions is to provide them with opportunities for regular ethical exercise' (Doel *et al.* 2010, p.1884).

The GSCC's guidance on professional boundaries (2011) provides a helpful resource (see Further reading and resources section at the end of the chapter). It uses case material from conduct hearings to examine acceptable and unacceptable behaviour and the possible impact of such behaviour on service users, as well as on upholding public trust and confidence.

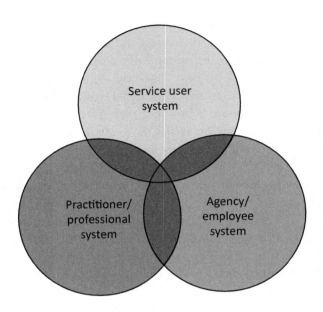

Figure 4.1 The boundaries and 'shadows' in social work

Points to consider

- Is your relationship focused on promoting the well being of the service user?

- Are your personal needs being met through contact with the service user?

- Has the service user ever behaved in a way that suggests that they have misunderstood your professional relationship?

- Is your relationship with the service user, their friends or family adversely influencing your professional judgement?

- Is the relationship you are having with the service user, their friends and their family a professional one? If not, have you made your employer aware of this?

(GSCC 2011, p.11)

The following case example is taken from the GSCC (2011, p.16) guidance, as are the points to consider that follow.

Case study

The social worker was employed as a team manager in a fostering team. Whilst working in this role, the team manager engaged in a number of activities with looked-after children whose cases were allocated to members of his team. His actions included:

- taking a child to a football match

- taking a child out for a meal

- taking a number of children swimming

- buying a child an X-box

- paying a child to clean his car

- taking a child to his home address.

There was no professional reason for any of these actions – they were not part of any care plan and had not been discussed with the allocated social worker. The team manager did not record these actions in the relevant care files and did not inform his own manager about them.

Points to consider

- Why is this behaviour misconduct?

- Would any of these actions have been acceptable if they had been undertaken by the looked-after children's social worker? Why?

- What potential impact could the team manager's actions have on the children concerned, their friends and family?

- Why might it have been important for the team manager to have discussed his actions with his employer?

- Why might the team manager's failure to record these actions be significant?

- Which aspect of social work values have been breached in this example?

- Which part of the regulator's standards for the profession might have been breached in this example?

(GSCC 2011, p.16)

There may be times when it is service users who misconstrue the boundaries of a professional relationship, or they may initiate some inappropriate action. Nevertheless, it remains the social worker's responsibility to ensure that the social worker's role is clearly understood and that they act in the best interest of the service user. And it is to the service user's perspective that we now turn.

What do service users want?

As usual, we finally have a chance to speak – in the 'graveyard' slot.

(Anonymous service user in a training session)

The above comment was made by a service user giving a presentation in a training session. The session had been timed to empower service users by giving them the final slot (and metaphorically, the final say) but, as can be seen, this intention was clearly misconstrued. It reflects the difficulty of enabling service users to speak in a way that is empowering and meaningful for them, without it appearing tokenistic.

A frequent complaint by parents whose children have been placed in care is that if they had access to some of the resources it took to keep their child in care, they would be able to make significant and substantial changes in their lives and so remove the need for social work involvement. The fact that the foster carer may not be able to manage their child's behaviour, may be of an inappropriate religious, cultural or racial match, and so be unable to fully meet their child's needs, may also exacerbate these feelings. Understandably, what service users want most is to be empowered to be autonomous – and free of social work support.

Oliver (2010), in her review of children's views and experiences of their contact with social workers, concluded that social workers and young people had very different ideas of what it meant to listen. For young people, listening involved the social worker acting on what the young person had said to them and responding accordingly. For social workers, listening was much more a process that involved having 'an attitude of respect and awareness' of the young person's feelings (Oliver 2010, p.46) but within the constraints of their post. It was noted that some positions legally required the social worker to prioritise the young person's welfare over and above their explicit wishes and feelings.

Similarly, older people suffering from abuse from family members may want the abuse to stop, but perhaps not at the expense of other (perceived greater) losses that this may entail, such as the loss of emotional support and connection with loved ones (Donovan and Regehr 2010). Such factors present a challenge to social workers in working with service users; balancing service users wishes with ensuring they are safeguarded and that they meet their own social worker professional obligations.

Case study

Gardener (2008, p.41) describes working with Colin, a man in his 60s who had been left with severe cognitive impairment and very little speech after a motorbike accident:

> Colin had been indicating for some time that he was thinking of moving out of his home. His relationship with his partner, Mary, had not been entirely easy before his motorbike accident, and he felt it had broken down further since then... Colin asked me to support him in discussing this with Mary. At the meeting, she said that she would not stand in Colin's way, but that she feared a move would increase his sense of isolation and would be counter-productive. She became agitated and angry with Colin as she thought about the practical and financial implications for herself and their daughter. Colin himself appeared increasingly distressed and tearful and eventually indicated that he had changed his mind and no longer wished to move.

What would your professional response be in this situation?

How could the service user's wishes be respected?

One of the things that service users value is the quality of the relationship they have with their social worker. This is an area where social workers can have some influence. Doel (2010) found that service users value:

- understanding the intentions and purposes of the worker

- being able to contribute to the work of the service

- receiving help speedily

- the worker's ability to respond to feelings that they may not always express

- the worker's concern and attention, even if change is not possible
- the worker's ability to exercise care, even when exercising control.

(Doel 2010)

Whilst this shows that service users value 'reciprocity' in their relationships with social workers, this does not mean that they are unaware of the imbalances of power between them, or even between the worker and their agency. It therefore follows that how the social worker is experiencing their professional power and using it in their work will have an important impact on the quality of their relationships with service users.

Power

Social workers can struggle with the authority they hold. It can feel overwhelming to walk into a stranger's home and to know that your assessment could decide, for example, whether they have the capacity to make their own decisions, or will be forced into receiving medical treatment against their wishes, or what, if any, services they may be entitled to. Feelings of frustration and helplessness can result when a worker has made painstaking efforts to conduct an assessment whose recommendations are then simply rejected, leading, conversely, to feelings of powerlessness.

> Power? What power? My assessments are not worth the paper they are written on. I've lost count of the number of times I've been told there are no resources to meet the needs I've identified.
>
> (Anonymous social worker, quoted with permission)

This swinging pendulum illustrates the complex nature of power within social work. On the one hand, social workers have a lot of power and, on the other, it is tempered by organisational constraints. These may include being answerable to a line management structure, often working to bureaucratic regulations or may simply be resource led.

This can lead to a tendency to think in 'simplistic black and white terms (seeing people as either powerful or powerless)' (Thompson 2007, p.7) and for power to be seen as a bad thing without acknowledging the good it can do.

Some texts refer to seminal theories of power by philosophers such as Max Weber and Michel Foucault. This can make it difficult to take the concepts referred to and apply them to one's professional practice in a meaningful way. Therefore, the focus here will be on power as it relates to the professional social work role.

Thompson (2007) uses to the PCS (Personal, Cultural or Structural) model, to refer, not only to power, but also to the different types of discrimination people can experience in society. Personal, cultural and structural refer to the different levels at which power (and therefore discrimination) can operate. There will be a discussion about discrimination in the next chapter, so the focus in this section is on the different types of power.

Personal power (also referred to as psychological power or charisma) refers to an individual's capacity to achieve their own ends and can refer to attributes such as self-confidence, self-belief and resilience.

Cultural (or discursive) power refers to processes by which a consensus is developed over time. Thompson (2012) cites sexual division of labour as one example of this: the way a specific culture may attribute certain jobs to specific sexes.

Structural power refers to where a person may be located in the social hierarchy – either in the wider society in which they live, or in the organisation in which they work. For example, how resources are allocated (what are the criteria for who should receive a service and the thresholds for what they are entitled to?).

Thompson's model is useful in clarifying the different types of power and the context in which they can be relevant. Professionals may also wish to consider their own personal power in different aspects of their lives, and the way they use their professional power. Both of these will be considered next.

Personal power

Points to consider

Think about your workplace:

* Does everyone at the same level of the organisation have the same level of power?

- Or are there some practitioners who can exert a greater influence than others?

A worker may or may not have much charisma (or personal power) at work, but may be a respected and highly thought of member of their own community, within their extended or their nuclear family. This type of power can be context and situation specific.

Owen's (2008) audit of charismatic celebrities showed that they tended to have the following characteristics (see Table 4.1 for a full summary):

- Have high self-esteem: charismatic people tend to brim with self-confidence, inner calm, self-reliance and a sense of independence.

- Score highly on having a 'strong sense of purpose' and a strong sense of personal values that drive their behaviour consistently and strongly.

- Are emotionally intelligent: aware of their feelings and those of others.

- Have a strong vision of what they want and make it happen.

- Are full of energy: passionate, enthusiastic and committed.

How do you think you would score on the different aspects of your life?

Professional power

The extent to which social work has become a profession is a recurring question, as is the issue of whether or not social workers see themselves as 'experts' in their field (Baginsky et al. 2010).

Points to consider

- What different powers do you have in your current role?

- What are the limits to these powers?

- Are there some areas in which you are more comfortable to exercise your authority than others?

Table 4.1 Owen's Charisma or 'Symbol of Star Quality' model

1. High self-esteem – in other words self-confidence, inner calm, self-reliance, independence	Charismatic people have high self-esteem – which can be particular to an environment. This conveys confidence and authenticity. When you have high self-esteem you are relaxed about exposing your true self. Levels of self-esteem can vary with situation, so this element is one of several which is contextual. Self-esteem, and thereby charisma, can vary according to situation.
2. A driving force – in other words purpose, personal values, principles	Charismatic people have an underlying sense of purpose, a set of values – principles important to them – which drive their decisions and actions. Values and purpose help drive and motivate behaviour consistently and strongly, which others see to be dynamic and enthusiastic. A strong driving force can also be contextual. Many people are strongly driven and charismatic in a certain direction or field, but not in others.
3. Sensory awareness – in other words empathy, emotional intelligence	Charismatic people are aware of their own feelings and the feelings and moods of others. They are in touch with their emotions and are uninhibited about showing them. This makes them expressive and compelling in the way they communicate and engage with others.
4. A Vision – in other words visualisation, belief, mental picture, positive attitude towards aim	Charismatic people have a strong vision of what they want. This is different to driving force or purpose. The point here is the mental vision of the purpose. To imagine and believe the aim – to see it happening in your mind. This creates a strong energy of intent that others can feel, and often see and hear too. Positive attitudes help produce results. Having a strong mental picture of your aims tends to reinforce your own actions and the responses and actions of others in the direction of the vision.
5. High Energy – in other words passion, enthusiasm, commitment, determination	Exhibiting high personal positive energy builds and maintains a positive energetic response in others. Positive energy makes others feel good. They become energised, feel valued and productive, and so respond even more strongly to the source – the charismatic person.

Source: Nikki Owen's 'Symbol of Star Quality Model is © Nikki Owen and Audience with Charisma Ltd 2011, and is used with their kind permission

Thompson (2003) refers to the different ways language can be used to oppress and to empower service users. He refers to factors such as jargon, using language that is stereotyping, and so de-personalising service users; as well as the use of 'exclusive' language. (e.g. using words such as 'chairman' instead of 'chairperson'). Whilst it could be argued that such words are simply common parlance, it is also worth considering the impact that these words have in continuing to marginalise some members of society and, as in this example, imply that 'women do not belong to positions of power' (Thompson 2003, p71).

Points to consider

- Study a recent report you wrote. How many times do you:
  - use jargon
  - make stereotypical statements
  - use words that could be stigmatising
  - use 'exclusive' language (such as 'chairman' rather than 'chairperson')
  - use language that depersonalises service users?
- How aware are you of such 'lapses' in the reports of other colleagues or professionals?
- How easy would it be for you to challenge them?

Power to, power over, power with and power within

Professionals have the *power to* achieve positive outcomes for service users, as well as having *power over* them. They have the *power* to work *with* (*power with*) people to encourage collaboration and partnership working so that service users can develop the *power within* themselves, drawing on their resilience and inner strength.

These four terms relating to power (power to, power over, power with and power within) are often discussed in literature regarding the ethics of power. Some of the debates can be multi-layered and complex, but they are mentioned here as it is useful for social workers to be aware of the different ways that power can be used within their role. Power can be used as a tool to protect, oppress, or collude with service users, as well as to work co-operatively with them. Table 4.2 gives an example of each of these.

Table 4.2 Examples of different types of power relations

	Power over	Power together
Positive modes of power	**Protective power**	**Co-operative power**
	Example: Using statutory powers to safeguard vulnerable people	Example: Working alongside service users and empowering them to take positive action
Limiting modes of power	**Oppressive power**	**Collusive power**
	Example: Exploiting one's own position and access to resources to enhance one's own position at the expense of others	Example: Working with one or more people in a way that oppresses or excludes others

Source: Adapted from Tew (2006)

Tew (2006) points out that there is 'still little consensus as to what power actually is' and that the term 'empowerment' is used to either refer to 'mutual support' or to refer to people deemed to be 'powerless' by 'powerful' politicians or professionals. He offers an approach which illustrates the shifting and complex nature of power. The following case study builds on Tew's reference to domestic violence to illustrate the shifting nature of power.

Case study

Siobhan suffered from domestic violence for a number of years, from her male partner, Regan. Police were frequently called to the family home, more so after the birth of their second child. After a recent serious assault, a social worker, Neil became involved.

He encouraged Siobhan to leave. She was temporarily placed in a women's refuge.

The scenario is further explored in Table 4.3, which shows how various responses from the different people involved relate to the different types of power. It is a fluid concept that continually changes.

Table 4.3 How different people in the case study could use different types of power at different times

	Power over	Power together
Productive modes of power	**Protective power** Neil encouraging Siobhan to leave abusive relationship. Neil referring Regan on so he gets the appropriate support from an organisation that works with perpetrators of violence (men's group). Siobhan could leave her partner or ask him to leave their home, to protect herself and her children from the effects of further violence.	**Co-operative power** Siobhan working with Neil to protect her children. Siobhan building supportive and enabling relationships with other women in the women's refuge. Neil working co-operatively with Siobhan and with Regan to ensure each gets the help they need and that their children are safeguarded. Regan agreeing to attend a men's group for perpetrators of violence.
Limiting modes of power	**Oppressive power** Neil developing an oppressive relationship with Regan (treating him as a pariah). Regan continuing to be emotionally and physically violent to Siobhan.	**Collusive power** Siobhan and Regan's ongoing relationship where neither takes responsibility for their actions. Siobhan developing collusive relationships with other women in the refuge based on a 'shared victimhood'. Neil developing a collusive relationship with Siobhan (treating her as a victim and colluding with her apparent helplessness). Regan colluding with other members of the men's group as he does not see the point in attending. Siobhan returning to live with Regan without any of the issues having been resolved.

Tew's model of power shows vividly how power can shift from moment to moment and how a social worker, if they are not careful, can move from a place of acting protectively to acting oppressively; or from a place of acting co-operatively to acting collusively and so on. Even working protectively (which could be perceived as being helpful) can be experienced by service users as being paternalistic or may, in time, create a dependency. There may, of course, be times when the law requires social workers to take specific actions. The challenge then is how these actions can be carried out without oppressing or colluding with service users or with other professionals.

Much of the time, however, social workers will encounter ethical dilemmas in their practice when they are working in a one to one situation with service users. The remainder of this chapter will look at ethical dilemmas in practice, specifically focusing on issues concerning boundaries, the use of power and managerialism.

Ethical dilemmas in practice

Increasing managerialism within the profession has meant that most significant decisions and tasks are now decided by managers. The reasons for this may seem clear: to make decision making less biased and more transparent, to ensure accountability, to minimise discriminatory and oppressive practices and to ensure that practice remains ethical, within the law and within the professional code of practice (Banks 2011). However, this may have the unintended consequence of social workers not having the opportunity to develop their ability to reflect on and analyse the work they do. There is the added danger that, by simply following procedures, social workers become cut off from their personal and professional values.

In most cases social workers (or their managers) will make a decision based on their statutory obligations (what the law says they must do); the policy requirements of their organisation; criteria set around who can receive what service (e.g. criteria for who is entitled to an assessment) and on the resources available (e.g. which social workers are available to do an emergency home visit; what resources are available if a placement is needed urgently).

Nevertheless, there are areas of practice where social workers may be faced with a moral or ethical dilemma that falls through these categories and can still have a profound impact on service users.

Points to consider

Have you ever:

- avoided or minimised your intervention with an abusive service user?
- been over-generous with the time/resources/financial help you give some service users whilst being overly stringent with others, because of how you felt about them?
- been judgemental about a service user because you don't approve of their culture or lifestyle?
- realised, with hindsight, that you had been overly optimistic in your work with a service user because you liked them or got on well with them?

Thompson (cited in Haverkamp and Daniluk 1993) distinguishes between three different types of ethical dilemmas: those that are *ethical but illegal* (e.g. the social worker who decides not to report a paedophile who is already convicted and in prison on separate offences, because of concerns about how it will impact on the child they are working with); those that are *unethical and illegal* (such as failing to report abuse because the worker is unaware of the procedures and does not look them up) and those that are *unethical and legal* (such as working with families where abuse has occurred without the appropriate training, knowledge or expertise). All of these combinations exert a powerful influence on practice.

Professional codes are useful in setting the parameters of ethical conduct, but tend to focus on general guidelines of behaviour rather than giving specific advice on which values or principles have priority when there are competing ones (Mattison 2000). The way in which a social worker responds may depend on the way they (or their manager/organisation they work for) perceive and interpret their different priorities, according to the law, organisational policy and procedures on those issues (see the values matrix, Figure 1.1).

Yet in each case there are also some areas of grey, which are areas of interpretation, which relate to *how* an assessment of a situation was carried out.

Research has shown that decision making is done in different ways by different professionals. Some work intuitively, whilst others critically evaluate the different options available (Kitchener, cited in Haverkamp and Daniluk 1993). Kitchener suggests practitioners turn to the following six ethical principles as a guide to ethical decision making. These are based on and build on Beauchamp and Childress' principles of biomedical ethics (2009), which are discussed in Chapter 2:

Autonomy: How important is it that the service user is able to make a free and independent decision?

Beneficence: This is the principle to 'do good'. Will the outcome of the decision enable this?

Non-maleficence: This is the principle to avoid harm. To what extent is this possible? A vulnerable child or adult may already be suffering some sort of harm, but is the social worker likely to cause further harm (albeit in a different way)?

Justice: How far can everyone in the scenario be treated fairly and equally?

Fidelity: Can the professional do what they say they will do?

Self-interest: Is there any aspect of this decision that could impact negatively on the social worker (e.g. does this decision go against their own personal morals and values)? If so, how will this impact on what they say or do to the service user? How can they attend to their own needs, without this interfering with their work?

Case studies

Have a look at the following scenarios. Can you see which ethical principles apply in each one?

- Jessie has been working with Beth for several months. Beth is a heroin user and was referred to the Drug and Alcohol Team by Children's Services as her children are currently being looked after by foster carers. Beth was previously a child in care herself. Jessie has been struggling to build some kind of relationship with her but Beth has not been co-operating with her, nor participating fully in the rehab programme. Jessie is worried about Beth losing her children and has therefore spent a lot of time trying to build a relationship with her. This has been at the expense of staying focused on the issues around her addiction. Should Jessie refocus her priorities or will Beth simply experience this as yet another oppressive professional in her life?

- A Youth Offending Social Worker, Stephan, becomes aware that a young person is continuing their offending behaviour. Stephan needs to ensure that young people take responsibility for their criminal behaviour, but also that there is due regard for their general welfare. He is not sure whether custody is the most effective response for ensuring someone abides by a court order. Should he return to court or not?

- Bernice is assessing a young Asian disabled woman who asks her not to disclose to her family that she wishes to leave home and live independently. Bernice knows that her parents will not approve of such a decision, and it is culturally frowned upon. Does she tell her that she can only work in an open and transparent way and go against her wishes, or does she respect the service user's rights and lie to the family, insisting it is her social work assessment that they are unable to provide the young woman with the care needed (when this is not true)?

It could be argued that the six ethical principles are so fundamental, that all of them could apply to all three scenarios. A couple of principles are looked at for illustrative purposes, for each scenario.

Jessie could rationalise her actions (in spending a lot of time trying to build a relationship with Beth, at the expense of looking at her addiction issues) by arguing that she was seeking to assess her motivation to change, or to lay firm foundations before she went on to do more challenging work. However, in this case, she is aware of feeling overwhelmed with the amount of power she wields and, as a mother herself, is feeling extremely uncomfortable about contributing in any way to another mother losing her children. These feelings are preventing her from actually working with Beth in an effective way.

In terms of ethical principles, it could be argued that Jessie is not acting with fidelity as she has been avoiding discussion around Beth's addiction. Also, the principle of self-interest is significant, as Jessie's personal values (belief about families remaining together) is impacting on her ability to work with Beth and also her ability to work with other professionals around safeguarding Beth's children.

Stephan may know that his organisation's procedures require him to return to court. However, experience has taught him that custody is frequently not the answer for young people, and does not meet their welfare needs, nor is it helpful in preventing further offending. If Stephan feels that his actions may cause, rather than prevent, further harm, this will lead him to either question why he is working in his current position, or he will shut a part of himself down, and work to the organisation's procedures on 'auto pilot'.

Stephan appears to be weighing up the principles of beneficence (doing good) versus non-maleficence (avoiding harm). His role may be to prevent reoffending in young people, but he is concerned about the harm caused by custodial sentences. If these concerns lead Stephan to question the 'fit' between his personal values and professional duties, then the principle of self-interest would also apply.

Bernice's response will depend, in part, on how comfortable she is with the power attached to her role, and how confident she is in exercising it sensitively. It would be easy for her to feel protective towards the young woman (especially if she feels that her religion and culture are oppressive), and so collude with her wishes. If she does this, it will mean also lying to her employers and effectively going against her professional codes (HCPC 2012). To work effectively and co-operatively, Bernice could discuss with the young woman her anxieties about telling her parents she wishes to leave home and how she could be enabled to move forward.

The principles of autonomy and justice offer interesting perspectives to Bernice. On the one hand, she has to assess to what extent the young woman has the right to make a free and independent decision (autonomy). Does this right extend to lying on her behalf and/or causing harm to herself and/or others? To what extent does Bernice have a duty to treat everyone she works with equally (with justice)? What does 'equal' mean in this context? As lying for a service user would undoubtedly have a negative effect for Bernice, the principle of self-interest would apply. This would be compounded if Bernice believes that the young woman is living in a household where the religion and culture is oppressive.

As mentioned earlier, one of the factors that determines the way in which social workers carry out their duties is whether or not they believe they are behaving in line with their personal as well as their professional values. It is interesting to note that in each of the scenarios the practitioner experiences a clash between their personal values and their professional duties. How these conflicts are resolved, or indeed, the level of insight that the practitioner has about them, will determine their impact on practice. It is at times like this that social workers need good supervision, with a manager who is trusted, who can provide a 'sounding board', insight and ideas around resolving the conflict (Wonnacott 2012). Having someone who can hold your practice to account and, with tact, point out where your personal values may be colouring your assessment is invaluable, as is someone who can actively listen and acknowledge what tough choices have to be made in an imperfect world.

The idea that practitioners' decision making is influenced by their cultural background and beliefs is not a new one. Mattison's work (2000) in this area is worthy of note. He refers to the need to make stereotypes and biases explicit and for social workers to be 'ethically aware' of their individual, ethical stances. Mattison goes on to develop several useful paradigms around ethical decision making. One of these, a decision making questionnaire, has been adapted below. The purpose of this is to help practitioners think about the factors that influence their decision making; to make these more explicit, so that they are then able to make ethically based decisions in an informed way.

Questionnaire: What is your approach to tackling ethical dilemmas?

Think of a difficult decision that you had to make in relation to one of your cases and answer the following questions:

1. To what extent did my personal views or beliefs influence the decision? (These could be your beliefs about the service user's culture, religion, sexuality, gender, disability, or it could be the impact of your own family of origin, your politics, etc.)

- I was aware of my personal biases or preferences and attempted to keep these from unduly influencing the outcome.

- I had not considered the extent to which my personal values may have influenced the ultimate decision.

2. To what extent did legal obligations influence my decision in this case?

- Not at all.

- Somewhat.

- It was a deciding factor in my decision.

3. Was I willing to act beyond legal (statutory) obligations, if doing so meant serving the service user's best interests?

- No. My statutory obligations took priority.

- Yes. If the law does not meet the service user's needs, I will try to find another way in which they can be met.

4. To what extent did adhering to my employer's policies influence my decision in this case?

- Not at all.

- Somewhat.

- It was a deciding factor in my decision.

5. If my employer's policies conflicted with the needs of the service user, was I willing to act outside of these policies?

- No. My first obligation is to my employer.

- Yes. There are times when I will fight for the rights of service users, even if doing so means going against my employer's policies.

6. To what extent did my role in the organisation influence my decision? (Do you believe that your decision might be different if you held another position? For example, if you were a social worker in another team, or a manager?)

- My decision was strongly influenced by my role.
- My decision was somewhat influenced by my role.
- I would have made the same decision regardless of my role in the organisation.

7. If the case involved a conflict between a service user making a decision (self-determination) or you making a decision on their behalf (paternalism), which did you prioritise?

- The service user being able to make their own decision was the priority.
- The service user's decision was secondary to my professional judgement regarding what I believed to be the right course of action.

8. In making a decision, the deciding factor for me was:

- Evaluating the possible costs and benefits of the various courses of action to the service user and their family.
- Strictly adhering to the law, and to my employer's policies and procedures.

(Adapted from Mattison 2000)

Points to consider

What order of priority did you give the following:

- your personal values
- legal obligations
- your employer's policies
- your role in the organisation.

Did you prioritise service users' wishes or your professional assessment of their situation? Was this appropriate?

Conclusion

This chapter has mapped some of the ethical issues involved in working with service users. Basic building blocks around direct work have been revisited and examined: how professional boundaries are defined in direct work; how social workers use or have the potential to misuse the power they hold; the limits of that power and the way in which power can shift. Different types of ethical dilemmas have been discussed and also different styles of decision making.

A number of ethical dilemmas were looked at based on the principles approach outlined in Chapter 2 (see the matrix of ethical theories, Figure 2.4). Readers are also referred to the values matrix (Figure 1.1), to the interaction of personal and professional values with one's duties to one's professional codes of conduct, law, organisational policy and procedures.

It can be seen how Jessie, Stephan and Bernice respond to service users is also a result of their ability to reflect on their situation (reflective practice) and their commitment to anti-discriminatory practice.

For some, completing the ethical dilemmas questionnaire will reaffirm their commitment in putting service users first. For others, it may be sobering to realise how often other obligations (to the law, or organisational procedures) have a priority over what resources service users can access. What did the questionnaire indicate about your ethical decision making?

The next chapter builds on this one by providing tools to enable practitioners to develop greater self-awareness of their 'self' and the impact they can have on service users. This includes working with 'sameness' and 'difference'.

Further reading and resources

GSCC (2011) *Professional Boundaries: Guidance for Social Workers.* Available online at www.gscc.org.uk/cmsFiles/Conduct/GSCC_Professional_Boundaries_guidance_2011.pdf, accessed on 18 August 2012.

Owen, N. (2011) Symbol of Star Quality Model. Copyright Nikki Owen and Audience with Charisma Ltd. Sevenoaks.

Thompson, N. (2007) *Power and Empowerment.* Lyme Regis: Russell House Publishing.

Wonnacott, J. (2012) *Mastering Supervision.* London: Jessica Kingsley Publishers.

CHAPTER 5

Tools to Develop Self-Awareness

> ### Key messages
>
> - A positive relationship between worker and service user can account for up to 30 per cent of change for service users.
>
> - Practitioners use of 'self' is a fundamental part of their 'toolkit' and enables them to develop a better understanding of their interactions with others.
>
> - It is as important to acknowledge similarities as well as the differences in social location between a worker and service user, and the impact that this can have.

It is on your own self-knowledge and experience that the knowledge and experience of everything else depends.

(Anonymous, *The Cloude of Unknowyng*, fourteenth century CE)

Introduction

This chapter focuses on the two lower segments of the values matrix (Figure 1.1) – reflective and anti-discriminatory practice. As the above quote suggests, the focus is on developing greater self-awareness, especially in interactions that take place in direct work with service users.

As practitioners gather experience and develop their professional 'toolkit', many learn quickly that developing themselves, their 'people skills', is as important as developing a sound knowledge base, or experience of legislation, policies and procedures. This chapter explores some of this terrain. It begins with a discussion of the role of emotional intelligence, and other concepts that will enable workers to further build on the idea of the 'self' as outlined in the previous chapter. Although the concepts discussed are not uncommon in practice, they can be used without a full or appropriate understanding and so have limited application. The discussion then moves on to look at tools to enable workers to analyse aspects of interactions with service users; issues of 'sameness' and 'difference' in the social location of practitioners and service users, and how an understanding of both is required to enable practice to be truly anti-oppressive.

In terms of ethical theory, virtue ethics and the ethics of care are the theories that support this discussion. Virtue ethics focuses on the traits needed to be a good social worker, whilst the ethics of care focuses on the nature and quality of the relationship between worker and service user (see the matrix of ethical theories, Figure 2.4). If social workers are the most essential item in their own toolkits, they need to ensure they are the best social worker they can be. This includes being able to engage with people who do not want any contact with them, much less to *engage* with them. A workers ability to do this will depend, in part, on the level of emotional intelligence they have.

Emotional intelligence

Ideas around emotional intelligence have become popular in recent years – the work of Daniel Goleman (2006), for example, has led to the term becoming a common international one. Morrison (2007) looked at the concept of emotional intelligence within a social work context. He referred to 'intrapersonal' intelligence (how aware you are of yourself; and how you manage yourself) and to 'interpersonal' intelligence (your awareness of others and how you manage your relationship with them). Figure 5.1 shows this paradigm.

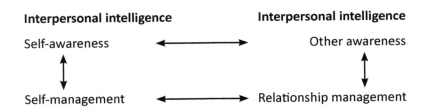

Figure 5.1 The emotional intelligence paradigm

Morrison used research by McKeown (2000) to show that the factors that are most likely to contribute towards change are the extent to which the social worker is able to understand and assess the relevant characteristics of the service user (things like the impact of their history on their current situation, their support network) and the extent that he or she is able to establish a 'purposeful relationship' with them. These factors combine to account for 70 per cent of the change. He argues that perception of emotion cannot be separated out from the assessment process (see Figure 5.2).

> Needs cannot be elicited or addressed without an appreciation of their emotional and cultural meaning. The result is that workers may see the need, but not the meaning of the need. In failing to elicit the meaning, well intentioned plans may fail.
>
> (Morrison 2007, p.255)

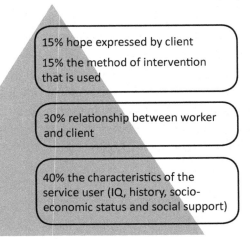

Figure 5.2 The main factors contributing to change in work with service users

A worker's capacity to empathise with a service user, to understand the nuances of what is said and what is left unsaid, will be affected by their ability to make sense of all the emotions in the room – their own and others.

Using the 'self' as a container

The concepts of 'the self' and 'containment' were referred to in Chapter 3, as was the importance of social workers developing skills to feel confident in *holding* or managing their own emotions. There are many occasions when social workers are also placed in a position of *containing others'* emotions, especially those of service users. These concepts will be further discussed and developed here.

Think about how you are at work, on a daily basis. Do you generally go home and continue thinking about work – someone you are working with that is giving you particular cause for concern, or do you leave work at the office? Are you easily affected by the emotion of distressed service users, or have you distanced yourself from such emotions, simply going in to work and get the job done? You may feel you have found a healthy balance, or that you know what a healthy balance is and are striving towards it.

If you could store all your emotions in a large container, what kind of container would it be? How thick would the walls be? How would you decide what emotions could go into the container and what could be left out? You could, for example, have a very porous container that easily lets in other people's emotions and also lets a lot of your emotions out of it. This could feel confusing as everyone's emotions would get mixed up in your pot, making it difficult to distinguish between your own or other peoples' emotions. Or you could have a watertight container, with a solid lid, that doesn't let anything in from the outside. That would mean that all your emotions stayed on the inside. It would also mean that, over time, you would become disconnected from those around you, as you would be out of touch with how they were feeling and they with you.

Of course, we cannot choose the kind of metaphorical container we are but we can work within the constraints of that container. We can develop an understanding of our own emotions, learn to tune into others' emotions and try to make sense of the interplay of both.

Emotions in and of themselves are simply a type of feedback. It is how we make sense of them that determines how useful they are in a professional context.

Briggs (1995) uses the concept of container in discussing the different interactions between a mother and her baby. A baby is crying. His mother responds to him. He is in a different place (emotionally) as a result of his mother's interaction with him. Briggs describes three different types of interactions that can take place, each is described as a different type of container: concave, flat or convex.

How the mother responds to the cries of her baby will, to some extent, depend on her own state of mind. If she is receptive and can *hold* the baby's emotions and tend to them, that might be enough to comfort the baby and let him know that he has been heard. When the mother is behaving as a concave container, she has the capacity to take in the baby's emotions and to *hold* them. What is important in this interaction is that the mother gives emotions back to the baby in a way that is manageable for him.

If the mother is depressed and feeling flat, she may not have the capacity to take in her child's emotions. These are not received and held, but are ignored, or simply left (flat container). If this goes on for a prolonged period, the baby will learn that there is no point in crying as his needs will not be attended to.

Being a convex container involves the mother initiating an interaction with the baby, rather than receiving and responding to one. She is letting the baby know her own state of mind. Briggs felt that this included positive interactions, as well as those that could be experienced as intrusive and distressing by the baby, but noted that they were more likely to be the latter. A small baby has not yet built up a capacity to contend with additional, especially distressing, emotions.

Figure 5.3 shows the different types of containers diagrammatically. The idea of an interaction with another representing a type of container can easily be applied to direct work with service users. Social workers frequently have to contend with situations where service users simply cannot manage their emotions. If the social worker is feeling flat, or overwhelmed, they will have a limited capacity to respond in a meaningful way, to discuss the situation in a way that makes sense and provides the appropriate information.

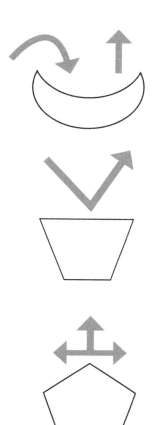

Concave container
There is capacity to receive, process and digest an interaction and to respond in a way that is meaningful to the person who receives it.

Flat container
There is no capacity to make sense of or digest emotions. They are simply returned to the giver, or are left to diffuse.

Convex container
Interaction is initiated with the other. This may be positive, but could also be the passing on of distressing or overwhelming feelings.

Figure 5.3 Examples of concave, flat and convex containers

This model is also helpful for practitioners in identifying what state of mind the service user is in, and their ability to take in important, perhaps distressing information. If the response is negative, and especially if it is hostile, strong feelings will be forcefully put into the social worker. Knowing that their client is acting as a 'convex container' may not make the situation any more bearable, but does provide a useful framework to understand their distress. If the social worker is able to respond by remaining calm, listening to their concerns and answering their questions in a way that can be understood, they have, in effect, *held* those feelings (acted as a concave container).

Points to consider

- How do you respond to difficult or hostile service users?
- What strategies do you use to establish a working relationship despite apparent lack of co-operation?
- How do you ensure the full co-operation of a service user you think may be showing disguised compliance?

Understanding projection, transference and counter-transference

Other concepts that may be useful for practitioners to understand or revisit are projection, transference and counter-transference. Howe (2009) offers accessible definitions and examples shown in Table 5.1.

Table 5.1 Definitions and examples of some common psychoanalytic terms

Term	Definition	Example
Projection	When we attack or ridicule some else for feelings that unconsciously bother us.	The man who is hostile to gay men because he may harbour uncertainties about his own sexual orientation. He attacks in others that bit of himself that causes him anxiety.
Transference	Feelings are transferred from one key relationship from the client's past or present on to the social worker.	If a client felt rejected by her father during childhood, she may unconsciously cast the social worker as rejecting...as if he was the rejecting father.
Counter-transference	Occurs when workers find themselves thinking and feeling about a patient in a distinctive and pronounced way.	A father who doesn't say much, makes the worker feel guilty (as he has unresolved issues regarding his own father).

Mastering the use of such concepts will provide an excellent basis for being able to separate out your own emotional 'stuff' from that of others. In fact, anything that helps you to be more attuned to your own emotions, those of the people you work with and the interplay of both, will enable you to be more emotionally literate.

Working with service users: Digging deeper

Case study

Paul, a black social worker, describes being yelled at, in front of his colleagues, by a white mother, to put down her baby:

> 'I felt miserable...humiliated... It was so sudden. I wasn't expecting that. It came...as a shock. Yeah, for this mom to say that she doesn't want a black man to be holding a white baby.' (Yan 2008, p.324)

On this occasion, the remark was about race. It could just as easily have been a homophobic or ageist remark (derogatory comments about the social worker being gay, or too young, for example). To say such remarks are shocking or unacceptable would, perhaps, be stating the obvious and would offer little consolation to the practitioner at the receiving end of such abuse. At such a juncture, Thompson's (2012) PCS model may offer intellectual understanding but perhaps not the tools to move forward.

One way forward may be to take stock of the situation (see Figure 5.4). This may involve making a list of some of the thoughts you may both be having (see Table 5.2).

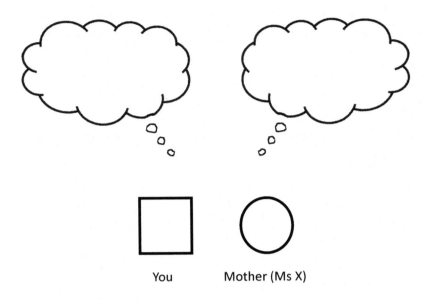

Figure 5.4 Putting yourself in another's position

Table 5.2 Listing your own thoughts and anticipating others'

My thoughts	Ms X

If you were in Paul's position, consider the different types of thoughts you may be having. How would they fit into the categories in Table 5.3? Can you think of any other categories?

Table 5.3 Categorising thoughts

Me	Ms X
How I see myself (e.g. being black (gay…young) is OK	**How Ms X sees me**
How I see Ms X (e.g. I am seeing red at the moment!)	**How Ms X sees herself**
How I think Ms X sees me (e.g. as someone who is less than her)	**How Ms X thinks I see her**
How I want Ms X to see me (e.g. as a human being and as a professional who is here to do a job)	**How Ms X wants me to see her**

An additional one for Paul may be:

How can I reframe these thoughts to:

- enable me to make a 'professional' response to Ms X

- enable me to carry out my professional duties.

It can be seen that the smallest encounter can be multi-faceted and based, by necessity, on what you think the other person may think about you or a particular issue. At best, you cannot really know what Ms X thinks or feels (only she knows that) but you can form a personal opinion, or a professional assessment based on your perception of Ms X, her verbal and non-verbal behaviour.

Whilst we can choose our personal relationships and hope that they are based on trust, mutual respect and honesty, this is not necessarily the case in a professional–client relationship. A service user may or may not want to receive a service. They may wish to avoid or influence a particular outcome (such as avoiding going into a residential home, or preventing their children from being taken away from them) and so may say or do things to influence your assessment.

Points to consider

- What impact do you think you have on service users?
- How do you take this into account in your work with them?
- How aware are you of the impact that service users have on you?
- Are you able to acknowledge your personal biases and prejudices, and the possible impact they could have on your work?

So, returning to the social workers toolkit, ensuring that you are emotionally literate, and have an understanding of your own and an ability to 'read' others' emotional responses is a good start to stocking up the toolkit. Another trait that is invaluable is having an awareness of your own social location (your sex, age, gender, etc.) and that of the person you are working with, and the interplay of both: that is how 'same' or 'different' you are from the service users you work with and the meaning you both attach to this.

Working with 'difference' and 'sameness'

Approaches to working with 'difference' (or diversity) have necessarily changed and developed over time. Depending on when and where you did your training, you will be familiar with different ways of looking at yourself and the way you work with service users who may be the same as you in some ways and very different to you in others.

In the 1960s and 1970s, the idea of western society as a 'melting pot' gave way to a more general awareness of 'ethnic minorities' and their cultural needs. This shifted towards cultural pluralism in the 1980s, the need to understand how identity develops in people from different backgrounds. The early 1990s saw the culmination of politicised anti-racist social work education, aiming to promote ethnically and culturally sensitive practice. This was followed by a move towards discussing 'diversity', acknowledging the multiple differences in society such as age, gender, sexual orientation, varying mental and physical abilities, as well as race.

Kohli, Huber and Faul (2010) and Gupta *et al.* (2011) offer interesting analyses of these trends. The latter note that social work educators in the UK have tended to prefer the 'more politically infused' term of anti-discriminatory or anti-oppressive practice over the apparently more neutral one of 'cultural competence' (Gupta *et al.* 2011, p.2). Cultural competence has been more prevalent in the United States. It implies that professionals have become competent in working with people from a range of different backgrounds. Cross (1998) presented a 'process' model, implying that there were definite stages one went through in attaining 'cultural competence'. These were cultural destructiveness, cultural incapacity, cultural blindness, cultural pre-competence, cultural competence and advanced cultural competence.

Although Cross was referring to 'culture' within a trans-racial context when the model was devised, Kohli *et al.* (2010) use the model within the broadest definition of the word, to encompass race, gender, sexuality, religion, mental and physical abilities and so on. This highlights the growing complexity in this area. They cite research by Sue *et al.* (1998) that details a cultural competency framework for counsellors, stating that it is transferable to a social work setting. Cultural competency is linked to practitioners having a good awareness of their own cultural values and biases, a good understanding of the world view of the service users they are working with and the ability to be able to intervene in a culturally appropriate way.

The focus therefore continues to be on understanding the nature of discrimination and working in a way that ensures that service users are not discriminated against. This approach tends to focus on 'difference' and assumes that as long as the social worker is aware of issues around diversity and discrimination, these will be minimised as much as possible. However, this does not take into account the interactive nature of 'sameness' as well as 'difference'. Both have an impact on the service user–professional relationship.

Understanding the impact of the 'self' on working with difference and sameness

1. Working with 'difference'

There have been few studies that have looked at the identity of professionals and the impact that this could have on their practice. Akhtar (1992) looked at the training of black social work students, and their subsequent entry into the profession. She found that black students entering social work training and then employment had additional barriers to cross, due to the eurocentric basis of social work training and of the profession itself.

It is inevitable that social work in the UK is based on western values (such as the emphasis on the rights of the service user – client autonomy). Not all of these values will be equally compatible with other cultures – especially those that emphasise collectivism. It follows that social workers from other cultures may have more difficulty adapting to western cultures than workers who are indigenous and already identified with them. In addition, practitioners may be more likely to have difficulty adapting to organisational values if those values do not fit in with their personal values.

Yan (2008) offers more up to date research. She looked at the cultural tensions in cross-cultural social work. This involved looking at cultural similarities and differences between social workers and service users, between social workers and the organisation they worked for, and finally, between service users and the organisation. Figure 5.5 shows the points at which tensions are likely to arise.

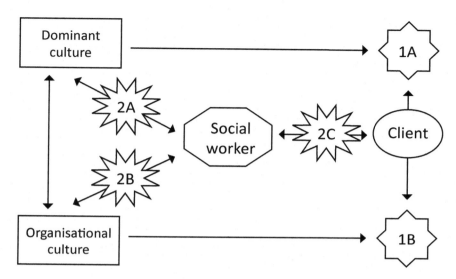

Figure 5.5 Cultural tensions in social work practice
Source: Yan (2008, p.321)

It can be seen that both service users and social workers from minority cultures can struggle with some aspects of the dominant culture. This is symbolised by the use of the numbering 1A and 2A in Figure 5.5. Service users and social workers from minority cultures can also struggle to understand the culture of large organisations (including the range of statutory health and social care settings). This is symbolised by the numbering 1B and 2B in Figure 5.5. An example of each kind of tension is given in Table 5.4 as a way of illustrating the types of difficulties experienced.

In addition, social workers may clash with service users. This is symbolised by the numbering 2C in Figure 5.5. Yan (2008) found that the area of most conflict tended to be around social workers' direct work with service users. Whether a worker had the same cultural background as the service user, or a different one, either combination had its complexities. Many workers suffered direct (e.g. not wanting a black social worker) or indirect racism (e.g. saying they could not understand their accent) from clients who were of a different cultural background to themselves.

Table 5.4 Examples of different types of tensions experienced by service users and social workers

CLASH	Service users (1)	Social workers (2)
Dominant culture (A)	**Example of 1A** Elderly parents of a mentally ill man cannot understand why a social worker is arranging for their son to live in a shared group home when it is against their wishes and they are more than happy to continue caring for him.	**Example of 2A** Social workers from minority cultures (especially those that value collectivism) may have difficulty understanding why children of an older person refuse to care for their parent.
Organisational culture (B)	**Example of 1B** A single mother with six children needs adapted accommodation so she can better care for two disabled children. She is told that as such housing is at a premium, her adult children will be offered bedsit accommodation. This effectively breaks up the family unit. The 'system' cannot accommodate the family's cultural needs.	**Example of 2B** A children's social worker has to refer a child to the Adoption Team. This presents her with an anathema as the concept of adoption violates her own cultural beliefs (such as the deep rooted nature of connections to one's family of origin).

2. Working with 'sameness'

Interestingly, being of the same cultural background as one's service user was found to also have its complexities. There were the obvious benefits. Workers generally saw this as an asset, as their shared cultural background enabled them to understand the service user's needs. It was described as a 'special bond' that generated mutual understanding.

However, there were also some significant difficulties. For example, depending on the culture or the situation, some workers were treated as members of the family and were invited to dinner or family functions. Service users were offended and could not understand a refusal. Yan (2008) found that Chinese families were less likely to co-operate with Chinese social workers, due to a belief that they would not be able to advocate as aggressively on their behalf as a social worker from another (indigenous?) culture.

Some workers commented on the 'transference' (see Table 5.1 for a definition of this) from families, who saw them as having 'sold out' or betrayed their own culture. Social workers' counter-transference was also more likely to be triggered, especially if they had had similar experiences to the people they were working with, as well as a similar cultural background.

Some of these findings replicate Thomas's (1992) exploration of racism and the therapeutic relationship. He noted that black patients receiving treatment from a black therapist could feel cheated, as they felt that black was not as good. There could also be hidden envy, especially if they suffered from low self-esteem and saw the therapist as someone who prospered professionally.

Being a black social worker can create a multitude of tensions with service users. Yan (2008) concluded that black social workers 'walk along an extra-fine line between personal and professional domains' (p.326) and, as a result, many often worked extra hard to prove their professional competence.

If this is so, then what are the implications of such findings for white social workers?

3. Understanding 'difference' and 'sameness' from a white perspective

> I feel totally excluded and left out. I am not black. I am not from a working class background. I am straight. I don't want to feel guilty about this and I just don't get it.
>
> (Anonymous social work student)

This quote indicates some of the frustration that some white social workers can feel around issues of racism in particular, and more generally around sameness and difference. Ryde (2009) offers a useful reframing of this experience and many of the points raised in this section arise from her work.

> When I started my research, I noticed how hard it is to focus on 'whiteness' as it seemed like looking at nothingness.
>
> (Ryde 2009, p.2)

Ryde's quest for greater understanding about 'being white' led her to ask the following questions, which you may wish to consider. She also connected with a 'prevailing sense of guilt and shame' in connecting with the 'privilege of whiteness'.

- Who am I as a white person?

- What is the nature of my privilege as a white person?

- How does being white affect my ability to relate to people who are not white?

- What is the nature of race?

- Who am I in a racialised environment?

> (Ryde 2009, p.3)

Jeyasingham and Morton (2009) also refer to the concept of 'white privilege' (and privilege and heterosexuality). Both refer to Peggy McIntosh's (1998) work in identifying 46 ways in which she benefited from being white. These include examples such as seeing one's own race represented widely on TV and in the press and never being asked to speak up for all the people in one's race.

Ryde goes on to develop a model describing the white person's struggle to understand racism (see Figure 5.6). It shows how moving from a place of denial, to frustration, in trying to understand discrimination, can lead to feelings of guilt and shame at being 'complicit in white privilege' (Ryde 2009, p.52). Unless this is attended to, it can lead to feelings of 'stuckness', and helplessness which can be overcome through questioning and engaging with issues around racism and the wider society we live in.

Coming to terms with these issues can lead to 'integration' where the 'self' is able to relate to issues of racism in an authentic way, without defensiveness.

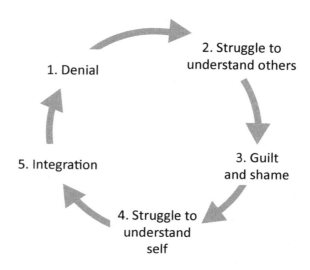

Figure 5.6 Cycle of white awareness
Source: Ryde (2009, p.50)

4. Diversity awareness

It could be argued that Ryde's model could have parallels with practitioners from all races and back grounds confronting different aspects of their personal prejudices. This links to the more overarching issues around diversity and cultural competence.

Gast and Patmore (2012) offer a 'Diversity Awareness Model' that can be used by practitioners, irrespective of their personal and social location (see Figure 5.7). Readers wishing to explore this further can do so in the *Mastering Approaches to Diversity in Social Work* book of this series by Linda Gast and Anne Patmore.

However, some caution does need to be exercised in looking at issues of diversity. Such a term implies 'all forms of discrimination and oppression are equal in their frequency, pervasiveness and intensity for both the individual and for society' (Graham and Schiele 2010, p.236). In a sense, this defuses the effects of any one kind of oppression, and also simplifies the complex interplay of discrimination within society. For example, poverty is more likely to disproportionately affect people with disabilities or people from ethnic minorities. The generic use of the term diversity can imply that all oppressions are 'equal' and not particular to context or time.

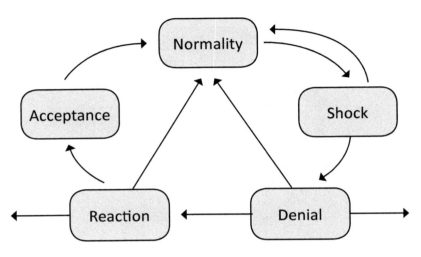

Figure 5.7 A diversity awareness model
Source: Gast and Patmore (2012)

Critical race theory appears to address this issue. It originated in American law schools in the 1980s as a politicised reaction to a colour blind criminal justice system. It is based on the premise that there are inequalities within society that need to be acknowledged. Although the theory was initially about race, it has subsequently been broadened out to include all social inequalities (such as class, gender, sexual orientation, religion, ethnicity, disability, educational achievement and residential status). Inequalities are socially constructed, and have a differing impact on people, based on where different aspects of their identities intersect with dominant culture. There is recognition of the impact of multiple oppressions and also that not all oppressions are equal.

The additional usefulness of this theory is the acknowledgement that social location is in itself part of the story; that to make sense of an individual's social location it is important to know about their lived experiences, and how they have come to make sense of different aspects of their identities and how they intersect with other dominant and subordinate cultures. Ortiz and Jani (2010) provide a helpful summary of the theory.

Critical race theory's understanding of complexity fits in well with the idea of 'complex accountability' (Clark 2000), discussed in Chapter 1, and reaffirms the need for social workers to be able to reflect on their practice, in an emotionally literate way, to make sense of service users' life stories and to ensure their practice is anti-oppressive.

However, these skills are not easy to acquire. So, to conclude this chapter, a final tool is introduced, which provides an opportunity for workers to build on their capacity to reflect on their direct work, in a detailed, step by step way: by conducting a 'process recording'.

Doing a process recording involves initially recording verbatim, and in as much detail as you can remember, a specific segment of an interview you have had with a service user. This will include verbal and non-verbal communication. Next, you add your thoughts and feelings at the time, at each significant moment. Finally, you step back, reflect on what happened and analyse the interactions in as much detail as possible.

Figure 5.8 shows the format for a process recording. Completing a process recording does require some planning and forethought – for example, it is important to choose a time and interview where you will have a few minutes to record what happened immediately afterwards (rather than leaving it until the evening or the next day). You may wish to share your recording with your line manager, practice educator, work colleague or a mentor, to maximise your learning. Repeated use of process recordings will build up your observation skills, and your ability to analyse your interactions, as well as other people's.

Process recording

Name: Date:

Background information:

Reason for meeting:

Name (who is speaking)	What is said (verbally and non-verbally)	Social worker's thoughts and feelings	Analysis	Practice educator's comments

Figure 5.8 Format for process recordings

Conclusion

This chapter has provided a range of tools to enable practitioners to further develop their ability to reflect and work in an anti-discriminatory way. These tools have ranged from enabling a focus on the minutiae of interpersonal interactions to the recognition of the structural inequalities in society and how these shape our perception and experience of the world.

The focus has been on the interpersonal – on direct work with service users. Although the chapter has not described a series of ethical dilemmas and worked through them, in the way some readers may have expected, there has been the implicit recognition that how one manages and makes sense of emotions in the social work encounter will enable one to be a more reflective practitioner who is better able to make sense of competing needs, rights and demands: everyday ethical issues.

How one responds to issues of discrimination and oppression is also an ethical issue. By working with the models presented in this chapter, workers can develop greater awareness of their sense of 'self', the most essential item in their social work toolkit.

Further reading and resources

Gast, L. and Patmore, A. (2012) *Mastering Approaches to Diversity in Social Work.* London: Jessica Kingsley Publishers.

Goleman, D. (2006) *Emotional Intelligence: Why It Can Matter More than IQ.* New York: Bantam Dell.

Howe, D. (2009) *A Brief Introduction to Social Work Theory.* London: Palgrave Macmillian.

Ryde, R. (2009) *Being White in the Helping Professions.* London: Jessica Kingsley Publishers.

CHAPTER 6

Ethical Issues in the Workplace

Key messages

- A key skill to becoming an effective practitioner is to understand the wider context of the organisation one works in.

- This involves beginning to think in a more analytical way about one's work and the impact of the wider organisation on it.

- Tools are offered to enable practitioners to develop a greater understanding of aspects of their relationship with their line manager, with team dynamics and ethical issues within the wider organisation.

- Details are given on how whistleblowing – reporting on misconduct – can be done via a third party.

Quotes from three social workers:

'I don't want to be set up as the "trouble maker" of the team – those rolling eyes…'

'I have no problem advising service users to seek legal advice and request a judicial review.'

'Those who shout the loudest will get a service. I will always fight for service users' rights and access to resources.'

Introduction

This chapter builds on the previous ones by exploring ethical issues in the workplace; relating to working with your manager, team and the wider organisation.

Having worked hard to establish a positive working relationship with a service user, and spent time carrying out a detailed assessment of their needs, it can be disheartening to be told that resources are not available to meet those needs. Practitioners pass on decisions that they may or may not agree with, from managers within their agency to service users. They may have tried hard to fight for a specific resource and then had to face the challenge of explaining to the service user why this cannot be accessed. This sense of constantly having to fight for limited resources causes stress, as well as raising ethical dilemmas for practitioners. There may also be a concern about service users becoming dependent on the services that are provided. The above quotes highlight different attitudes that workers can develop in response to such dilemmas.

As workers become adept at working within specific procedures and policies, their awareness of the limitations of those systems also becomes greater. Social work training places a strong emphasis on working within an anti-oppressive framework, so it may be unsettling to discover that some social work agencies can be hostile, oppressive places to work in. Even agencies that pride themselves on their transparency and good practice will inevitably have structural or institutional issues that create ethical or value based dilemmas for staff. (For a more detailed discussion about power, see Chapter 4 for a discussion of Thompson's 2012 PCS model.)

A key skill is to be able to understand the wider context of the organisation that one works in, and to be able to work within some of its limitations to achieve the best possible outcome for service users. This involves beginning to think in a more strategic way about one's work and the impact of the wider organisation on it.

This chapter looks at possible dilemmas faced within the workplace and offers tools to enable practitioners to reflect on their relationship with their line manager, their team and the organisation they are working in, to enable them to develop a greater understanding of this aspect of their working lives. There will also be an exploration of what to do when things go wrong and you believe that a colleague is behaving in an unethical and illegal way and that your employers are not taking any action.

As in the last chapter, this corresponds to the lower branches of the values matrix (reflective practice and anti-discriminatory practice; see Figure 1.1). In terms of ethical theory, the dilemmas faced are often between doing one's duty (what is the right, the just course of action; how can people be treated equitably?) and between balancing the needs of the few (usually individual workers or service users) with the needs of the majority (the team or the wider organisation). These relate respectively to deontology, utilitarianism and to the principles of justice and non-maleficence (see Figure 2.4 for the matrix of ethical theories).

To begin with, some tools are offered to enable workers to reflect on the organisation they work in and to locate themselves within it.

Locating yourself within the organisation

As Fook *et al.*'s (2000) research showed (in Chapter 3), over time, practitioners become more aware of the organisation in which they work. Health and social care settings can be highly structured and bureaucratic places with strong lines of accountability. This has positive benefits (such as knowing who to go to and when) but can also lead to frustrations and inefficiency (having to go through a number of long-winded procedures to achieve an apparently simple and straightforward task, such as getting a small amount of funding approved).

As practitioners become more experienced, their awareness of the strengths and limitations of their organisation will improve.

Case study

Spencer was excited about joining a busy inner city team that covered a deprived area. He was looking forward to the challenge of working with people with 'real problems' and making a difference to their lives. His friends had cautioned him about coming to this office, saying that it had a 'bad reputation' for having 'heavy' and high caseloads and that he would be better off working elsewhere. Spencer liked the idea of being challenged and had therefore accepted the post.

He was fortunate to have an excellent manager who provided the right mixture of support and guidance. This created a positive working environment for the whole team.

However, over time, Spencer became aware of issues that made him feel uneasy. For example, he had a suspicion that cases were not allocated equitably within the team. It soon became clear that a few workers were regularly allocated the 'heaviest' and most complex cases, whilst other workers seemed to retain a 'light' caseload. When Spencer raised this issue with his manager, he was told that cases were allocated according to the needs of the service user and also to the best worker to meet those needs. At first Spencer was flattered by this as it implied that his manager considered him a capable and competent. However, as the daily pressure of a constantly heavy workload took over his life, he reconsidered this view. He came to the realisation that some workers in the team were consistently underperforming and that his manager (for whatever reason) was unable to do anything about it.

Spencer's experiences are helpful in clarifying a number of points and will be further developed throughout this chapter.

First, organisations are not simply huge autonomous machines – they are living, breathing, complex systems. People or sections are intimately inter-related not only in the flow of work that passes through them, but also in terms of the lives of the people who work in them. Over time, individual workers, teams, or service areas develop reputations (which may or may not be accurate or based on any kind of 'truth') – such as 'that worker is hard working' or 'they don't do any work in that team'. These all combine to form the 'culture' of that organisation.

Harrison defines organisational culture as 'a set of norms, practices, ideas and beliefs about "how things ought to be done" in the organisation or a particular part of it' (Harrison 2000, p.135). Most social work agencies will have clear policies and procedures about what to do and when. Organisational culture can refer to the unsaid (perhaps even unconscious) practices, ideas and beliefs.

Points to consider

- Based on the information given, what are the positive and not so positive aspects of Spencer's team?

- How does this compare with the team you are currently working in?

Over time, Spencer discovers that although his manager is excellent in many respects, she has her limitations and also has areas that need further development – such as her ability to challenge poor performance. He also becomes aware of ethical issues within the wider workplace. These will be discussed later in this chapter.

In their review of adverse events in the health service, the Department of Health (2000) discuss the importance of creating a strong *informed* culture that consists of four important components:

1. a reporting culture (creating a climate where people feel able to report their errors or *near-misses*)

2. a just culture (this involves clear boundaries of what is acceptable and what is unacceptable behaviour in an organisation, but also the creation of a climate of trust)

3. a flexible culture (where skills of front line staff are respected)

4. a learning culture (where there is capacity to learn from errors without casting blame).

Consider your workplace. Figure 6.1 offers a model for thinking about the different aspects of the organisation you work in. You may wish to consider, what, in your view, is working well and what is not? What are the issues that leave you feeling 'uneasy'? How many of these have an ethical or unethical basis, or simply do not fit in with your personal or professional value base?

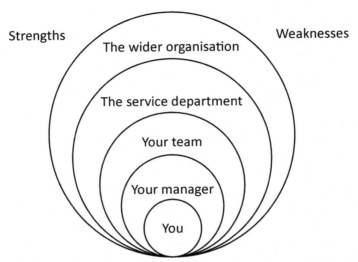

In your view, what works well and what does not?

Figure 6.1 Locating yourself within the wider organisational context

The remainder of this chapter will explore ethical issues within the contexts identified here: your relationship with your manager; with your team and the wider organisation.

You, your manager and supervision

The importance of good quality supervision is constantly highlighted within social work (Laming 2003; Munro 2011). Peach and Horner (2008) refer to the three main functions of supervision as educational (focusing on workers lack of understanding, knowledge and skills, as well as their attitude), supportive and administrative.

It has already been mentioned how, over time, Spencer became aware of his manager's limitations, as well as her strengths. This is not to imply that Spencer's practice was 'perfect' or that he did not have areas that he needed to further develop. It is also possible that Spencer's manager had sound reasons for her actions or inactions, but that he was not privy to this information due to confidentiality and professional boundaries. It is easy for workers to form an opinion about their line manager that can only be based on partial information.

It is not uncommon for workers to bring emotional preconceptions into the supervisory relationship which may be based on personal or professional factors such as their relationship with authority and previous (positive and negative) supervisory relationships (Wonnacott 2012). The reverse is also true, with managers doing the same. Table 6.1 summarises some of the factors that could influence the supervisory experience.

Table 6.1 Factors that may influence supervision

Factors	Influence on supervision
Halo effect	Where a worker is perceived as being very competent because they mirror or match their manager's self-concept (I am OK, so s/he is, too). This results in the worker being given a lot of autonomy over their work and little surveillance.
Horns effect	This is opposite to the halo effect. The manager perceives the worker as displaying worrying behaviour and so monitors them closely, offering very little autonomy.
Recency bias	This is where the worker's recent performance (positive or negative) overshadows the supervisor's perception of their overall performance.
Being 'other'	This is where the influence of race, ethnicity, gender, sexuality, age, disability, one's ideology or personality may lead to differences in understanding between supervisor and supervisee.
Being the 'same'	This is where the influence of the 'sameness' in race, ethnicity, gender, sexuality, age, disability, one's ideology or personality may lead to assumptions and collusion being made between supervisor and supervisee.

Source: Adapted from Peach and Horner (2008)

Points to consider

- How do you perceive your line manager's authority?
- To what extent is this based on:
  - their role?

- ○ your previous experiences of personal authority (e.g. parents, carers)?

- ○ your previous experiences of professional authority (supervisors, teachers)?

- ○ their (or your own) social location (age, race, class, gender, sexuality, disability)?

(Adapted from Wonnacott 2012)

It is also worth considering the conscious and unconscious 'games' that may be played out between you and your manager. Eric Berne (1964) described the 'games people play' in the book of the same name. He referred to people adopting one of three positions: the role of a parental figure, an adult or a child. Each of these roles represents an aspect of ourselves and becomes a stance that is taken in specific interactions. For example, a worker may be struggling with an issue (child state) and may repeatedly turn to their manager as a source of reassurance and emotional support (parent state). The manager in return can either respond in a way that reassures the worker and keeps them in a child state (parent–child); that is, one that keeps them emotionally dependent, or may respond in such a way that enables them to reflect on their practice and take responsibility for their own learning (adult–adult). All three states have productive and unproductive elements.

A similar model that is useful alongside Berne's is Karpman's drama triangle (1968) which also refers to three emotional states in interacting with people: the victim, rescuer and persecutor states. A manager addressing a practitioner's poor performance could be experienced as being persecuting by the worker, who may perceive themselves as a victim. The worker can seek solace or support through team members by complaining about their manager, putting them in the position of rescuers. What is interesting about the drama triangle, is how quickly positions can change or be reversed. The manager in the above example, could experience the social worker's response as persecuting, and may feel like a victim, turning to her line manager for support (rescuing).

The two models used together can provide a useful tool to reflect on supervisor/supervisee interactions – especially when it feels that things are not going well. If you are feeling 'got at' or persecuted by your manager, it is likely that you are in a 'child' state, and are not responding to them in a calm, adult manner. This is likely to escalate the situation, leading to you feeling victimised and bullied. If you can remain calm and in your 'adult' state, it is likely that your manager will also be able to switch into their adult state and respond to you in a more appropriate way (see Figure 6.2).

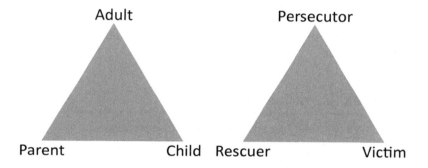

Figure 6.2 Working with the drama triangle: What 'games' are played between you and your supervisor?

Case study *continued*

Kiran was a social worker in Spencer's team. Although she had been there for nearly three years, she struggled to work effectively and frequently did not keep to important deadlines. Her record keeping was poor. Her manager had raised these issues with her several times. However, Kiran found herself getting anxious and overwhelmed, so was not able to 'hear' what was being said to her. She felt blamed and under attack and so was not able to understand what she needed to do differently. Consequently, Kiran had been telling other team members and colleagues about being bullied by their manager.

Her manager had not felt able to risk allocating complex or 'heavy' cases to Kiran and this had further undermined her confidence. Lately, Kiran felt de-skilled in her work and the quality of her work with service users had suffered.

A colleague introduced Kiran to the drama triangle. She realised that she felt persecuted by her manager and so became infantilised, unable to speak to her as an 'adult'. It was painful for her to acknowledge that there were areas in her practice that needed to improve. She rehearsed how she was going to discuss this issue with her manager. At her next supervision, Kiran focused on remaining calm, 'grounded' and tried to make points in a neutral way, without casting blame on anyone. She informed her manager that although they had discussed her performance before, that her high levels of anxiety had prevented her from fully understanding what she needed to do differently. This approach enabled Kiran's manager to respond as an 'adult' too. They set concrete targets that they both understood and that felt achievable.

Points to consider

- What 'games' do you play with your manager?
- What 'games' do you think your manager plays with you?
- What areas do you need to work on, or further develop, to ensure that you get the most out of supervision?

Kiran and Spencer offer different experiences of workers with the same manager and the same team. One was being protected from heavy, complex cases, whilst the other was being given more because it was seen that he was competent and able to manage them. This raises the ethical question: to what extent should all workers be treated equitably in a team in the number and complexity of cases given to them (principle of justice)? The team manager was unwilling to give complex cases to Kiran, presumably to avoid any harm (principle of non-maleficence).

It does seem reasonable that practitioners have an expectation of being treated the same as their peers. It is also clearly important to safeguard service users and ensure they are dealt with by competent workers. Perhaps the balance is in what contributions each worker makes to their team and if these collectively add value to the team, and enhance its ability to deal with its primary task – of meeting the needs of service users, as defined by the agency's policies. The next section explores some of the issues around team working.

You and your team

Teams can be a source of practical, emotional support, where colleagues can provide useful feedback, ideas and informal supervision around one's work. They can also be places of pessimism, where hidden agendas take over, leading to unhealthy downward spirals of negativity that stifle creativity and lead to fragmentation and distrust.

A team is any group of people who come together to work towards accomplishing a common purpose or goal (Finlay and Ballinger 2008). A social worker may be located in a team (such as a hospital discharge team or children with disabilities team) but will also be working with a range of other teams – literally a team around every service user, which may consist of social workers, managers, a range of other professionals, carers, members of the service user's family or community and, of course, the service user themselves. Although the discussion in this section focuses primarily on work-based teams (i.e. the team one is situated in), the tools and concepts presented here are designed to help you reflect on issues that may arise in teams, whatever their membership.

With 'hot-desking' being the norm, and the ability to work from home, or on a mobile basis, there are fewer opportunities for workers located in the same team to come together on a regular basis. This minimises opportunities for social workers to access valuable social and emotional support, which can act as a strong buffer against stress. Huffmeier and Hertel (2011) found that many cheers make light work – that the social support gained from team members was an important factor in the whole team's performance and outweighed any individual worker's performance. They distinguished between different types of support: teams where workers felt supported around receiving the right information at the right time and around specific tasks lead to greater productivity, and teams receiving social recognition and social encouragement lead to workers feeling more motivated.

Points to consider

- What are the norms in your team?

- In your view, are there some workers who are more advantaged than others?

- If some practitioners have more influence than others, why do you think this is?

The characteristics of effective teams

Figure 6.3 lists the characteristics of effective teams. You will not need to study the list too hard to know what an effective team is like. You will have a good sense of this already, as you will instinctively know what it feels like to be in an environment that feels positive, supportive, where dialogue happens easily, without fear or malice. Team members are encouraged to discuss and think through new ideas and to develop new skills. There is a positive relationship between supervisors and supervisees (Woodcock 1989).

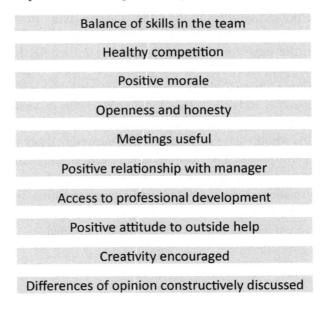

Balance of skills in the team

Healthy competition

Positive morale

Openness and honesty

Meetings useful

Positive relationship with manager

Access to professional development

Positive attitude to outside help

Creativity encouraged

Differences of opinion constructively discussed

Figure 6.3 Characteristics of effective teams

These positive aspects are the differences between a group and a team (Maddux and Wingfield 2003). In a group, workers work independently, and even at cross purposes with each other. They essentially do what they are told. There may be distrust and game playing. The focus is very much on the individual worker. This differs from a team, where the focus is on getting the job done, through interdependence and mutual support. Members of a team are willing to contribute to the team's overall objectives. Communication is open. That is not to say that there is no conflict. Rather differences are discussed and questions welcomed.

You may feel that, as a practitioner, you have little influence over some of the more powerful dynamics of your team. Your experience of your team may actually leave you feeling disempowered at times. Whatever your experience is, it is useful to consider the part you play in the team culture. The idea of different members of a team having different parts or roles to play will be explored in more detail shortly. However, there are teams in which social workers are very influential and have a vital part to play – the teams around service users – the multi-disciplinary, multi-agency teams that are created to meet the specific needs of service users. Often, it is social workers that play a key role in co-ordinating information and services and in ensuring that all the different team members co-operate fully to meet their responsibilities.

Social workers in such a position need to ensure that they focus on the quality of relationships they build with other professionals, as well as the tasks that each is expected to fulfil. (Gratton and Erickson 2007). If there are ongoing difficulties in ensuring collaboration, Maddux and Wingfield (2003, p.53) suggest seven steps to problem solving:

1. State what appears to be the problem.

2. Gather facts and feelings and opinions.

3. Restate the problem.

4. Identify alternate solutions.

5. Evaluate alternatives.

6. Implement the decision.

7. Evaluate the results.

Another model of team working is where a multi-disciplinary team is located within a central office – such as an intake or referral and assessment team. Team members from the various disciplines are responsible for jointly dealing with specific types of referrals. Teams located within hospitals, dealing with domestic abuse or safeguarding are common examples. Finlay and Ballinger (2008) explored whether these types of teams presented an effective way of working. They looked at commonplace assumptions about such teams and then identified the disadvantages. For example, one assumption is that such teams can deliver a comprehensive range of treatment and care services. However, they found that it can be confusing, perhaps even disempowering, to have many different disciplines offering advice, some of which could be contradictory, and that a negotiated division of labour can actually result in a less holistic service for service users, as no one may be attending to the overall package of care. Another assumption is that such teams present a cost-effective and efficient way of allocating resources. However, Finlay and Ballinger (2008) stated that such team work can prove to be inefficient and expensive, especially when team members do not communicate effectively. Inefficiency can arise if so many meetings are required that there is then no time to carry out the actual work.

The message here is that team working can have enormous benefits but can also be difficult to get right. Carpenter *et al.* (2003), for example, looked at social workers' experiences of working within multi-disciplinary mental health teams. They found that social workers had poorer perceptions of team functioning than other professionals in the same team, and that they also experienced higher role conflict. No analysis of the possible reasons behind this finding were offered, but it does appear that not all professionals in teams will be exposed to the same levels of stress and responsibility.

Team roles

Points to consider

- What part do you play in your team?
- What is your unique contribution?
- What are your strengths and weaknesses as a team player?

However you experience being in teams, it is inevitable that you play a part towards how that team functions as a whole. The idea of different members of a team having a crucial role to play has been developed further by Belbin (2004) into formalised 'team roles'. A team role is a 'tendency to behave, contribute and inter-relate with others in a particular way' (Belbin 2004, p.60). Belbin's research over many years has led to the identification of nine different role types within teams. That is not to say that a team needs to have nine members in it, as each member can adopt several roles, but it is helpful to have most of the team roles represented within a team, to ensure it functions effectively. It is likely that most members will behave according to one or two specific roles, have a medium score on a few roles and perhaps score very poorly on the rest. Team roles reflect one's personality, mental ability, values, motivations and experience. They are also dependent on the role occupied within a team. So, if you change teams and take on a significantly different role, it is possible that your role type score will also change. The team roles are listed and described in Table 6.2.

As well as the vital contribution that each team role possesses, they also have 'allowable weaknesses' that are the other side of their team role. It is helpful for all team members to have some awareness of their allowable weaknesses and to ensure that these are held in check. For example, team workers are sociable, but wish to avoid conflict, at all costs. So they may need to be alert to situations where important decisions need to be made that may involve conflict.

Table 6.2 Belbin team roles

Role	Description
Co-ordinator	These people inspire trust, confidence, are quick to spot others' strengths and so use them to further the groups interests. They may not be the cleverest people in the team but do have a tendency to win the respect of the team. (*Allowable weakness:* May delegate work to others. Need to be careful not to also delegate their own.)
Team worker	Team workers are sociable, flexible in their way of working and mindful of supporting others. They are perceptive and diplomatic and can work with sensitivity but do not like friction and will go to great lengths to avoid it. (*Allowable weakness:* May find it hard to make important decisions if this means having to choose one side over another.)
Shaper	Shapers are ambitious and highly motivated. They can present as extrovert and perhaps aggressively so with their drive to succeed. They can be competitive and can bring a lot of energy into a situation. (*Allowable weakness:* They can be direct and can offend people with their lack of insight.)
Plant	Plants are introverted, reacting strongly to praise and criticism, in equal measure. They can also be highly creative, generating ideas which can lead to major developments for the team. (*Allowable weakness:* They prefer to work alone so may not be at their best in a team situation.)
Resource investigator	Resource investigators love networking and making links with others, in and outside of the organisation. Outgoing, relaxed and inquisitive, they are natural negotiators. They are adept at developing ideas. (*Allowable weakness:* They can quickly lose interest as their attention is drawn to the next new thing. This can make them unreliable in completing projects.)

Implementer	Packed full of common sense, implementers have discipline and self-control. They are systematic in their thinking and approach, efficiently ensuring the job gets done. They have a strong sense of loyalty. (*Allowable weakness:* They can be slow in taking up new ideas and may lack spontaneity.)
Completer finisher	As their name suggests, this role type is adept at following things through and ensuring completion. They have a great eye for detail and can present as calm, even when they are filled with anxiety. (*Allowable weakness:* They tend to be shy and introverted.)
Monitor evaluator	Carefully weighing things up critically, monitor evaluators can be slow in making decisions but this means that they are rarely wrong. They have a huge capacity to excel in whatever they do. (*Allowable weakness:* They may present to others as boring.)
Specialist	Specialists are committed to their field and have little interest in others. They work hard to maintain professional standards, with great dedication. They can come to fill a unique role as no one else will have the breadth and depth of their specialist knowledge. (*Allowable weakness:* They tend to have little inclination to get involved in projects outside their area of expertise and so may come across as inflexible.)

Note: For more about Belbin team roles, check out www.Belbin.com.

Points to consider

- Which team roles do you identify with?

- What do you think your 'allowable weaknesses' are?

- Are there any serious weaknesses that stop you from being an effective team player?

This section has explored how team members can contribute to a team according to their team role, and according to their personalities and individual styles. However, there may be times when the functioning of a team may be affected by factors unrelated to its membership but more influenced by policies, procedures, wider and organisational issues. The next section discusses the use of systems theory and its contribution to understanding teams and organisations.

You and the wider organisation

Case study *continued*

Over time, Spencer learned that he had to amend and adapt his assessments around the services available within the organisation. These were not always appropriate to the service users' needs. Whilst staff were generally friendly and helpful, there were a number of procedures that were convoluted and, quite frankly, ineffective. He developed a sense of which teams worked well, and those which were plagued with inefficiency and 'difficult' workers. He and his colleagues would joke about a team who were never in a position to accept referrals and who simply did not appear to do any work.

Whatever your personal or professional values, whatever team you are in, the work you do will be defined by the wider organisation. This includes the policies, procedures, the style of the management team, the organisational culture. Stokes (2009, p.121) refers to all of these as the organisation 'in-the-mind'. Each worker from the same organisation will carry different views of that organisation. These may contradict each other but will influence how those workers interact with others, and will also contribute to the 'collective-organisation-in-the-mind' (p.121). This may include ideas about what the organisation says it does, what workers believe it actually does, and what may be being played out at an unconscious level (Lawrence, cited in Stokes 2009).

For example, the concept of a container was discussed in Chapter 5. It could be argued that institutions act as containers, 'holding' the difficult or unmanageable emotions of workers. Personal conflicts, jealousies, rivalries and frustrations can easily be projected onto other workers, other teams or parts of the 'system' (see continuing case study above). For example, front line workers (dealing with referrals and initial assessments can show disdain towards workers in other teams, who are seen as having a less stressful and easier working life. It is not until those same workers are nearing burn out and transfer to the teams they have envied, that they realise that the workload is equally high, and pressures although not as acute as on the front line, are different, yet comparable. They soon learn to project their frustrations and envy onto a new team or another part of the organisation.

Stokes (2009) argues that this projection of internal conflict has historically served to provide a focus for blame, keeping individuals or teams locked into unconscious roles within an organisation. However, the traditional stability of large organisations has been replaced by constant change and recurrent reorganisations. This has meant that the goalposts around where to project one's anxiety have also been shifting. As there is no longer an obvious container for tensions and anxiety, this has led to an increase in personal stress. Also, whereas tensions may previously have been managed by a whole team projecting their unmanageable feelings onto another team, or up or down the organisational hierarchy, the pace of current change makes this difficult to do. Stokes (2009) believes this has resulted in an increase in bullying in organisations.

Points to consider

- Which team or service do you 'love to hate'?
- What role do you think they have come to hold for the rest of the organisation?

You may also wish to refer to Figure 6.1 – is there anything you want to change about the strengths and weaknesses of the wider organisation?

Being able to reflect on the wider context of the organisation you work in will enable a more holistic understanding of your primary task – promoting the well being of the service users you work with. If you are better able to understand what you or your team collectively do with unmanageable feelings, this will make those feelings less potent, freeing you to become a more reflective practitioner. There may be occasions, however, when you hold information about a team member, or about the wider organisation, that you know to be unethical and illegal. On such an occasion you may have to consider whether or not to 'blow the whistle'.

Whistleblowing

Case study *continued*

Spencer had noticed that an administrator regularly returned from lunch late, and smelling of alcohol. He had mentioned this to his manager several months ago, but the situation persisted. He began to feel disillusioned and decided he would focus on doing the best job he could, within the area he could influence: his own caseload.

Eighteen months later, Spencer was a much more confident worker. He had attended a number of different courses, was adept in his role, at balancing his duties towards his employers with his responsibilities towards service users. He felt he was ready to move on, and to seek a more senior position.

He was disconcerted to hear that a practitioner with very little experience had been promoted to a management position. A colleague informed him that the worker in question was in a personal relationship with the manager who had interviewed her for the post. Moreover, that manager owned his own cleaning company and he had tendered the cleaning of the entire office to this company.

Discovering unethical or even illegal practice within one's workplace can be concerning, especially if it is being carried out by those in positions of authority. Perhaps this is more so in professions, such as social work, which have a strong emphasis on anti-discriminatory practice; on fighting social injustice. The normal way of reporting such concerns, especially in large, bureaucratic organisations, is to pass them on, via the line management structure.

The term whistleblowing refers to someone who informs on unethical, dishonest or illegal misconduct within their organisation. It is thought that the term originated from a New Jersey statute that encouraged people to report failures by trains to blow whistles as they were coming to a crossing. The railroad companies were subsequently fined and half of the money was given to the person who had reported the malpractice (Children's Commissioner for Wales 2003).

There are differences in people's attitudes towards 'ratting' or 'blowing the whistle' that will inevitably be influenced by one's class, culture, society and political climate. For example, compare life behind the iron curtain in Russia in the mid-1970s where there was an expectation that everyone would 'inform' on each other, and that failure to do so was a crime, with Latino or African American youth gang members where 'ratting' is punishable by death.

Points to consider

- Where would you draw the line?
- Is there a difference between what you would report in your personal and professional life?

Consider the factors listed in Table 6.3.

Table 6.3 Drawing the line: What would you report?

Personal views on...	Professional views on...
lying	fiddling expense claims
shoplifting	taking drugs whilst at work
benefit fraud	emailing pornography
witnessing a car accident	having sex with clients
witnessing a mugging	making regular, long personal phone calls at work
witnessing a murder	

Whatever your cultural background may be, as a social worker, there is a professional responsibility and expectation that you will report any kind of activity that places service users at risk (GSCC 2010). Failure to do so may be deemed gross misconduct by your employer but could also invalidate your registration as a registered social worker. It is also sobering to consider the position that vulnerable service users may find themselves in if it were not for professionals blowing the whistle.

There can be two different types of whistleblowing. The first involves workers raising concerns within one's own organisation. For most workers, this will involve discussing concerns with their line manager and then working their way up through the organisational hierarchy. For some, this may not be appropriate. The second form of whistleblowing involves taking the malpractice into a public forum, such as the press or, more usually, going straight to governmental bodies with one's concerns. The following are examples where workers did just that.

- A social worker speaking up about abuse and corruption in a North Wales children's home eventually led to the Waterhouse Inquiry.

- In 2009 an anonymous social worker disclosing malpractice in work with offenders in Edinburgh led to revelations of widespread corruption.

- It was a social care worker reporting the abuse of elders in a care home to managers and the Care Quality Commission that eventually led to an inquiry that showed widespread, shocking abuse taking place within the home.

For the whistleblower, whether or not to report misconduct is a moral dilemma. There is a conflict between doing one's duty and doing the right thing (i.e. reporting) on the one hand, and having a duty of loyalty to one's employer on the other (Lindblom 2007). Within social work, this becomes particularly important, as the dilemma also involves harm to others (often vulnerable service users), and to oneself, in the form of not being able to uphold one's professional code of ethics.

Reporting concerns about colleagues or one's employer takes courage. There may be concerns about not being believed, not being taken seriously, or about being discredited as a worker, and losing one's job. There is some reality to these concerns. The GSCC survey, for example, found that of those who reported a concern, nearly half found that no action at all was taken by their employer (Lombard 2009). Hunt, in his overview of whistleblowing within health and social care (Hunt 1995, 1998), also found, disconcertingly, that it was the whistleblowers who were likely to be vilified, rather than those they were reporting. One reason for this is that most organisations have clauses in their contracts and conditions of service around bringing them into disrepute.

Doel and Shardlow (2005) refer to factors that may 'push' a practitioner to report something and other factors that may 'pull' against disclosure. This is useful as not every issue that is encountered may be 'worth' reporting. Social workers are more likely to report malpractice if they have concerns about the well being and safeguarding of service users (Hunt 1995, 1998; Lewis and Homewood 2004).

Consider Spencer's experiences (outlined above). He informed his manager about an administrator who regularly returned from lunch smelling heavily of alcohol. Whether the manager took any action or not, the situation persisted. Spencer chose not to raise the issue again.

Points to consider

- What would you do in Spencer's position?
- Would your decision be different if it was a social worker or a manager that was drinking during office hours?
- What is your agency's policy about drug and alcohol use during office hours?

Spencer's position illustrates an interesting facet about organisational culture, and the extent to which bad or even dangerous practice becomes accepted as commonplace. Senge (2006) comments on this by referring to the parable of the boiled frog. If you throw a frog into a pot of boiling water, it will try to jump out. If, however, the water is lukewarm, the frog will relax and settle down. If the temperature is increased gently, it will become drowsy and will be completely unaware of the danger it is in. Gino and Bazerman (2009) refer to this as the slippery-slope effect. They argue that misconduct is more likely to go unnoticed when workers experience a gradual deterioration of ethical working over time, compared to abrupt changes.

In Spencer's case, he had already learned that drinking during office hours apparently went unchallenged and that workload allocation between workers was not shared equally. So, news of inexperienced workers gaining promotion on the basis of their personal relationships, and a senior manager exploiting a conflict of interest, rather than declaring it, was unsettling, but not surprising. It confirmed to him what he already suspected: that equal opportunity policies and working practices around anti-discriminatory practice were just that: paper polices that applied more to some workers than to others. If Spencer moved on and discovered similar unethical practices elsewhere, he might eventually accept such practice as unfortunate but 'normal'.

Such findings may present a stark picture for whistleblowers, especially as the GSCC placed a duty on social workers to report unsafe practices (GSCC 2010). In reality, however, practitioners may routinely raise concerns with their manager, or within their organisations, and these may be responded to in an entirely appropriate manner. It is helpful for workers to reflect on the general functioning of the team and organisation they work in, to develop an antenna as to its strengths and weaknesses. This will enable them to respond more effectively to meet the needs of the service users they are representing.

The Public Interest Disclosure Act (1998) was brought in to provide legal protection for the whistleblower and applies to employees wishing to report misconduct within their organisation. Areas that qualify for protection under the act include reporting:

- a criminal offence
- the breach of a legal obligation
- a miscarriage of justice
- a danger to the health or safety of an individual
- damage to the environment
- deliberate covering up of information tending to show any of the above five matters.

This applies to information relating to events that have taken place in the past, are happening now or are likely to happen in the future. The report on Standards in Public Life, Standards of Conduct in local Government in England, Scotland and Wales (also known as the Nolan Report 2001) recognised the important contribution which whistleblowing could make in countering inappropriate behaviour and ensuring high standards of probity. The report recommended that every local authority should introduce a procedure for whistleblowing. That view was accepted by the Government and has since been implemented by public organisations including those in health and social care.

If you are aware of serious concerns and need to discuss them, the Public Concern at Work website (available at www.pcaw.org.uk; helpline number 020 7404 6609) may be able to provide support and assistance.

Conclusion

This chapter has focused on ethical issues that can arise within an organisational context. This may be to do with your relationship with your line manager, within your team or the wider organisation. Although some examples have been given of ethical issues that arise at these levels, the discussion has been kept general to enable a broad discussion about processes that most practitioners will be able to identify with.

As practitioners move beyond their assessed and supported year in employment towards greater experience, they realise that simply knowing organisational policy and procedures is not enough. They need to understand some of the processes that occur in supervision, with their line manager, or in their team, or they need to understand what it is about specific workers (often their peers) that makes them far more influential in the organisation than others.

The tools in this chapter have been offered to enable workers to think beyond emotive responses to situations, which at first may appear grossly unjust. It is suggested that developing a more analytical approach to understanding such issues will contribute towards better outcomes for service users.

Finally, it is worth reiterating some of the issues explored in Chapter 3 around changing professional values. Ongoing changes within the social work landscape mean that practitioners will continue to have their personal and professional values challenged. Whilst professional codes of conduct and ethics provide general principles and guidelines, workers can only look *within* themselves to know if they are behaving with integrity. This is especially the case in hostile working environments. It is important to work with awareness of one's personal values and the impact that they have on practice, and that practice has on them.

Further reading and resources

Belbin Team Roles are discussed at www.Belbin.com, accessed 21 August 2012.

Lord Nolan (2001) *Standards in Public Life, Standards of Conduct in local Government in England, Scotland and Wales*. Crown Copyright. Available at www.public-standards.gov.uk.Library/OurWork/3rdInquiryReport.pdf, accessed 20 November 2012.

Obholzer, A. and Roberts, V. Z. (2009) *The Unconscious at Work: Individual and Organisational Stress in the Human Services*. London: Routledge.

Public Concern at Work website, www.pcaw.org.uk, accessed 21 August 2012 (helpline number 020 7404 6609), may be able to provide support and assistance.

CONCLUSION

As for me, all I know is that I know nothing...

(Socrates, cited by Plato in 'The Republic')

This book started with a quote from the Greek philosopher, Socrates, so it seems fitting to close with another from him. As practitioners, we can try to work with uncertainty, turbulence and risk. However comprehensive an assessment of a situation is, there will always be factors that are not known. Social workers try to minimise the effects of what they don't know, but still remain accountable for those decisions.

The concept of 'complex accountability' (Clark 2000) was explored in Chapter 1. It was noted that social workers have multiple accountabilities. As well as being accountable to service users, they are accountable to their line manager and the wider organisation, to their professional body and, of course, to themselves. In this last respect, it is also worth considering to what extent we are morally, as well as professionally, accountable for what we do.

There is danger, especially in uncertain and turbulent times, that social workers may develop a thick skin and 'tune out' more mundane ethical issues; perhaps like the frog in the pot of warm water (see Chapter 6) who is blissfully unaware that the temperature is gently rising and that it is being slowly boiled alive. Taking time out to review one's personal and professional values is a timely antidote.

The examples chosen in this book have focused on everyday ethical issues within practice, to encourage workers to review their daily experience at work, to enable them to develop greater mindfulness of such issues. It is hoped that these tools and exercises have provoked thought, discussion, or contributed towards reflection and critical thinking, whether that be in relation to themselves, their direct work with service users, their relationship with their line manager and their team, or the wider organisation in which they work.

Such a review may make practitioners more aware of the temperature in the room, so to speak, and to develop a more conscious awareness of the 'why' of what they do.

REFERENCES

Abbott, A. A. (1988) *Professional Choices: Values at Work*. Silver Spring, MD: National Association of Social Workers.

Abbott, A. A. (2003) 'A confirmatory factor analysis of the Professional Opinion Scale: A values assessment instrument.' *Research on Social Work Practice 13*, 5, 641–666.

Adams, K. (1993) *The Way of the Journal: A Journal Therapy Workbook for Healing*. Baltimore, MD: Sidran Press.

Ahmed, M. (2011) 'Professional boundaries.' *Children & Young People Now*. London: NCB.

Aivazyan, T. A., Zaitsev, V. P. and Yurenev, A. P. (1988) 'Autogenic training in the treatment and secondary prevention of essential hypertension: Five-year follow-up.' *Health Psychology 7*, 7, 201–8.

Akhtar, F. (1992) 'The experience of being a black social worker: Recruitment, training and social work practice.' MA dissertation, University of Sussex.

Aristotle (350 BCE) *Nicomachean Ethics.*

Baginsky, M., Moriarty, J., Manthorpe, J., Stevens, M., MacInnes, T. and Nagendran, T. (2010) *Social Workers Workload Survey: Messages from the Frontline*. London: Social Work Task Force.

Banks, S. (2006) *Ethics and Values in Social Work*. Basingstoke: Palgrave Macmillan.

Banks, S. (2009) 'Integrity in professional life: Issues of conduct, commitment and vapacity.' *British Journal of Social Work 40*, 7, 2168–2184.

Banks, S. (2011) 'Ethics in an age of austerity: Social work and the evolving New Public Management.' *Journal of Social Intervention: Theory and Practice 20*, 2, 5.

Banks, S. and Gallagher, A. (2009) *Ethics in Professional Life: Virtues for Health and Social Care*. Basingstoke: Palgrave Macmillan.

BASW (2012) *Codes of Practice*. Available at www.basw.co.uk/about/code-of-ethics, accessed 17 August 2012.

Beauchamp, T. L. and Childress, J. F. (2009) *Principles of Biomedical Ethics*, 6th edn. Oxford: Oxford University Press.

Beckett, C. (2002) *Human Growth and Development*. London: Sage.

Beckett, C, and Maynard, A. (2009) *Values and Ethics in Social Work*. London: Sage.

Belbin, M. (2004) *Management Teams: Why They Succeed and Why They Fail*. London: Butterworth Heinemann.

Bentham, J. (1789) *An Introduction to the Principles of Morals and Legislation.*

Berne, E. (1964) *Games People Play*. London: Ballantine Books.

Bradshaw, M. and Ellison, C. G. (2010) 'Financial hardship and psychological distress: Exploring the buffering effects of religion.' *Social Science & Medicine 71*, 1, 196–204.

Brechin, A. (2000) 'Introducing Critical Practice.' In A. Brechin, H. Brown and M. A. Eby (eds) *Critical Practice in Health and Social Care*. London: Sage.

Bride, B. E. (2007) 'Prevalence of secondary traumatic stress among social workers.' *Social Work 52*, 1, 63–70.

Briggs, S. (1995) 'From Subjectivity to Realism.' In M. Yelloly and M. Henkel (eds) *Learning and Teaching in Social Work*. London: Jessica Kingsley Publishers.

Cameron, J. (2002) *The Artist's Way*. London: Pan Books.

Care Standards Act (2000) available at www.legislation.gov.uk/ukpga/2000/14/contents, accessed 21 August 2012.

Carpenter, J., Schneider, J., Brandon, T. and Wooff, D. (2003) 'Working in multidisciplinary community mental health teams: The impact on social workers and health professionals of integrated mental health care.' *British Journal of Social Work 33*, 1081–1103.

Cherniss, C. (1995) *Beyond Burnout: Helping Teachers, Nurses, Therapists and Lawyers Recover from Stress and Disillusionment*. New York: Routledge

Children's Commissioner for Wales (2003) *Telling Concerns: Report of the Children's Commissioner for Wales' Review of the Operation of Complaints and Representations and Whistleblowing Procedures and Arrangements for the Provision of Children's Advocacy Services*. Swansea: Children's Commissioner for Wales.

Clark, C. L. (2000) *Social Work Ethics: Politics, Principles and Practice*. London: Palgrave.

Clifford, D. and Burke, B. (2009) *Anti-Oppressive Ethics and Values in Social Work*. London: Palgrave Macmillan.

Corey, M. and Corey, G. (1989) *Becoming a Helper*. Belmont, CA: Brooks/Cole Publishing.

Crenshaw, K. (1993) 'Mapping the margins: Intersectionality, identity politics and violence against women of colour.' *Stanford Law Review 43*, 1241–1299.

Cross, T. (1988) 'Cultural competence continuum.' *Focal Point*, the bulletin of The Research and Training Center on Family Support and Children's Mental Health, Portland State University (Fall). Available at http://nysccc.org/family-supports/transracial-transcultural/voices-of-professionals/cultural-competence-continuum, accessed 22 August 2012.

D'Cruz, H., Gillingham, P. and Melendez, S. (2007) 'Reflexivity, its meanings and relevance for social work: A critical review of the literature.' *British Journal of Social Work 37*, 1, 73–90.

Dalrymple, J. and Burke, B. (2003) *Anti-Oppressive Practice: Social Care and the Law*. Maidenhead: Open University Press.

Department of Health (2000) *An Organisation with a Memory: Report of an Expert Group on Learning from Adverse Events in the NHS*. London: Stationery Office.

Disbennett, L. (2007) 'The Values Game.' Available at www.coachlee.com/valugame/LongList.html, accessed 15 August 2012.

Doel, M. (2010) 'Service User Perspectives on Relationships.' In Ruch, G., Turney, D. and Ward, A. (eds) *Relationship Based Social Work: Getting to the Heart of Practice*. London: Jessica Kingsley Publishers.

Doel, M. and Shardlow, S. M. (2005) *Modern Social Work Practice*. Aldershot: Ashgate Publishing.

Doel, M., Allmark, P., Conway, P., Cowburn, M., Flynn, M., Nelson, P. and Tod, A. (2010) 'Professional boundaries: Crossing a line or entering the shadows?' *British Journal of Social Work 40*, 6, 1866–1889.

Donovan, K. and Regehr, C. (2010) 'Elder abuse: Clinical, ethical, and legal considerations in social work practice.' *Clinical Social Work Journal 38*, 2, 174–182.

Dreyfus, H. L. and Dreyfus, S. E. (1986) 'Mind over Machine: The Power of Human Intuition and Expertise in the Era of the Computer.' In J. Fook, M. Ryan and L. Hawkins (2000) *Professional Expertise: Practice, Theory and Education for Working in Uncertainty*. London: Whiting and Birch.

Finlay, L. and Ballinger, C. (2008) 'The Challenge of Working in Teams.' In S. Fraser and S. Matthews (eds) *The Critical Practitioner in Social Work and Health Care*. London: Sage.

Fook, J. and Askeland, G. A. (2007) 'Challenges of critical reflection: Nothing ventured, nothing gained.' *Social Work Education 26*, 5, 520–533.

Fook, J., Ryan, M. and Hawkins, L. (2000) *Professional Expertise: Practice, Theory and Education for Working in Uncertainty.* London: Whiting and Birch.

Gardener, A. (2008) 'Beyond Anti-Oppressive Practice in Social Work: Best Practice and the Ethical Use of Power in Adult Care.' In K. Jones, B. Cooper and H. Ferguson *Best Practice in Social Work: Critical Perspectives.* London: Palgrave Macmillan.

Gast, L. and Patmore, A. (2012) *Mastering Approaches to Diversity in Social Work.* London: Jessica Kingsley Publishers.

Gerber, M., Kellmann, M., Hartmann, T. and Pühse, U. (2010) 'Do exercise and fitness buffer against stress among Swiss police and emergency response service officers?' *Psychology of Sport & Exercise 11*, 4, 286–294.

Gilligan, C. (1993) *In a Different Voice: Psychological Theory and Women's Development.* London: Harvard University Press.

Gino, F. and Bazerman, M. H. (2009) 'When misconduct goes unnoticed: The acceptability of gradual erosion in others and ethical behaviour.' *Journal of Experimental Social Psychology 45*, 708–719.

Goleman, D. (2006) *Emotional Intelligence: Why It Can Matter More than IQ.* New York: Bantam Dell.

Goodwin, R. E. (1993) 'Utility and the Good'. In Singer, P. (ed.) *A Companion to Ethics.* Oxford: Blackwell.

Graham, M. and Schiele, J. H. (2010) 'Equality-of-oppressions and anti-discriminatory models in social work: Reflections from the USA and UK.' *European Journal of Social Work 13*, 2, 231–244.

Gratton, L. and Erickson, T. (2007) 'Eight ways to build collaborative teams.' *Harvard Business Review*, November, 101–110.

Greeno, W. J., Hughes, A. K., Hayward, A. and Parker, K. L. (2007) 'A confirmatory factor analysis of the Professional Opinion Scale.' *Research on Social Work Practice 17*, 482.

GSCC (2008) *Raising Standards: Social Work Conduct in England 2003–2008.* London: General Social Care Council.

GSCC (2010) 'A Duty to Whistle Blow'. Available at www.socialworkconnections.org.uk/features/202/a_duty_to_whistle_blow, accessed 16 October 2012.

GSCC (2011) *Professional Boundaries: Guidance for Social Workers.* London: General Social Care Council. Available at www.gscc.org.uk/cmsFiles/Conduct/GSCC_Professional_Boundaries_guidance_2011.pdf, accessed 22 August 2012.

Gupta, A., Fook, J., Bhatti-Sinclair, K., Hatzidimitriadou, E. and Yenn, L. (2011) *Informing the Development of Cultural and Ethical Competence in Social Work Education.* Report for SWAP (Social Policy and Social Work). Southampton: Higher Education Academy.

Harrison, K. and Ruch, G. (2008) 'Social Work and the Use of Self – on Becoming and Being a Social Worker.' In M. Lymbery and K. Postle (eds) *Social Work: A Companion to Learning.* London: Sage.

Harrison, R. (2000) *Employee Development.* London: Chartered Institute of Personnel and Development.

Haverkamp, B. and Daniluk, J. C. (1993) 'Child sexual abuse: Ethical issues for the family therapist.' *Family Relations 42*, 2, 134–139.

HCPC (2012) *Standards of Proficiency: Social Workers in England.* London: HCPC. Available at www.hpc-uk.org/assets/documents/10003B08Standardsofproficiency-SocialworkersinEngland.pdf, accessed 22 August 2012.

Holloway, M. and Moss, B. (2010) *Spirituality in Social Work.* Basingstoke: Palgrave Macmillan.

Howe, D. (1999) 'Values in Social Work.' In M. Davies, D. Howe and R. Kohli (eds) *Assessing Competence and Values in Social Work Practice.* Norwich: UEA Social Work Monographs.

Howe, D. (2009) *A Brief Introduction to Social Work Theory.* London: Palgrave Macmillan.

Huffmeier, J. and Hertel, G. (2011) 'Many cheers and light work: How social support triggers process gains in teams.' *Journal of Managerial Psychology 26*, 3, 185–204.

Hull, C. and Redfern, L. (1996) *Profiles and Portfolios: A Guide for Nurses and Midwives.* Basingstoke: Palgrave MacMillan.

Hunt, G. (1995) *Whistleblowing in the Health Service.* London. Edward Arnold.

Hunt, G (1998) *Whistleblowing in the Social Services.* London. Edward Arnold.

IFSW (2012) *Code of Ethics.* Available at www.ifsw.org/policies/statement-of-ethical-principles, accessed 14 February 2012.

Jeyasingham, D. and Morton, J. (2009) *Re-thinking Power and Oppression: The Uses and Limitations of Privilege.* Manchester: University of Salford.

Jones, S. (2009) *Critical Learning for Social Work Students.* Exeter: Learning Matters.

Kant, I. (1785) *Groundwork for the Metaphysics of Morals.*

Karpman, S. B. (1968) 'Fairy tales and script drama analysis.' *Transactional Analysis Bulletin 7*, 26, 39–43.

Klassen, J. (2004) *Tools of Transformation: Write Your Way to New Worlds of Possibility.* West Conshoshocken, PA: Infinity Publishing.

Kohlberg, L. (1984) *The Psychology of Moral Development.* London: Harper Row.

Kohli, H., Huber, R. and Faul, A. C. (2010) 'Historical and theoretical development of culturally competent social work practice.' *Journal of Teaching in Social Work 30*, 252–271.

Lai, H.-L. and Li, Y.-M. (2011) 'The effect of music on biochemical markers and self-perceived stress among first-line nurses: A randomized controlled crossover trial: Music reduces stress.' *Journal of Advanced Nursing 67*,11, 2414–2424.

Laming, Lord (2003) *The Victoria Climbié Inquiry Report.* London: Stationery Office.

Laming, Lord (2009) *The Protection of Children in England: A Progress Report.* London: Stationery Office.

Lewis, D. and Homewood, S. C. (2004) 'Five years of the Public Interest Disclosure Act in the UK: Are whistleblowers adequately protected?' *Webjournal of Current Legal Issues.* Available at http://webjcli.ncl.ac.uk/2004/issue5/dlewis5.html, accessed 23 August 2012.

Lewis, R. (2005) 'Kant 200 years on.' *Philosophy Now 49*, 4.

Lindblom, L. (2007) 'Dissolving the moral dilemma of whistleblowing.' *Journal of Business Ethics 76*, 4, 413–426.

Lombard, D. (2009) *Survey Reveals Doubts over Value of Whistleblowing. Community Care.* London: Reed Business Information.

MacIntyre, A. (1985) *After Virtue, a Study in Moral Theory.* London: Duckworth.

Maddux, R. B. and Wingfield, B. (2003) *Teambuilding: An Exercise in Leadership.* Menlo Park, CA: Crisp Publications.

Maslach, C. and Goldberg, J. (1998) 'Prevention of burnout: New perspectives.' *Applied and Preventative Psychology 7*, 63–74.

Mattison, M. (2000) 'Ethical decision making: The person in the process.' *Social Work 45*, 3, 201–212.

McIntosh, P. (1988) 'White Privilege and Male Privilege: A Personal Account of Coming to see Correspondences through Work with Women's Studies.' In M. L. Andersen and P. H. Collins (eds) *Race, Class and Gender: An Anthology.* Belmont, CA: Wadsworth.

McKeown, K. (2000) *A Guide to What Works in Family Support Services for Vulnerable Families.* Dublin: Department for Health and Children.

Mill, J. S. (1863) *Utilitarianism.* London: Parker, Son and Bourn.

Mill, J. S. (1869) *The Subjection of Women.* London: Longmans, Green, Reader and Dyer.

Mitchell, V. (2011) 'Professional Relationships.' In P. J. Barker (ed.) *Mental Health Ethics.* London: Routledge.

Morrison, T. (2007) 'Emotional intelligence, emotion and social work: Context, characteristics, complications and contribution.' *British Journal of Social Work 37,* 2, 245–263.

Munro, E. (2011) *The Munro Review of Child Protection: Final Report.* London: Stationery Office.

Nahum-Shani, I. and Bamberger, P. A. (2011) 'Explaining the variable effects of social support on work-based stressor–strain relations: The role of perceived pattern of support exchange.' *Organizational Behavior and Human Decision Processes 114,* 1, 49–63.

Narasimhan, L., Nagarathna, R. and Nagendra, H (2011) 'Effect of integrated yogic practices on positive and negative emotions in healthy adults.' *International Journal of Yoga 4,* 1, 13–19.

Nicolson, P., Bayne, R. and Owen, J. (2006) *Applied Psychology for Social Workers,* 3rd edn. Basingstoke: Palgrave Macmillan.

Oliver, C. (2010) *Children's Views and Experiences of their Contact with Social Workers: A Focused Review of the Evidence.* Leeds: Children's Workforce Development Council.

Ortiz, L. and Jani, J. (2010) 'Critical race theory: A transformational model for teaching diversity.' *Journal of Social Work Education 46,* 2, 175–193.

Owen, N. (2008) *The Charisma Elements Model.* Sevenoaks: Performance Practitioners. Available at www.businessballs.com/freespecialresources/Charisma_Report.pdf, accessed 23 August 2012.

Parrott, L. (2010) *Values and Ethics in Social Work Practice.* Exeter: Learning Matters.

Peach, J. and Horner, N. (2008) 'Using Supervision: Support or Surveillance?' In M. Lymbery and K. Postle (eds) *Social Work: A Companion to Learning.* London: Sage.

Perls, T. (2012) 'Life Expectancy Calculator.' Available at www.livingto100.com, accessed 17 August 2012.

Robbin, J. (2006) *Healthy at 100: The Scientifically Proven Secrets of the World's Healthiest and Longest-Lived Peoples.* New York: Random House.

Robinson, L. (2004) 'Beliefs, Values and Intercultural Communication.' In M. Robb, S. Barrett, C. Komaromy and R. Rogers (eds) *Communication, Relationships and Care: A Reader.* London: Routledge, Taylor and Francis.

Ross, W. D. (1930) *The Right and the Good.* Oxford: Oxford University Press.

Ryde, R. (2009) *Being White in the Helping Professions.* London: Jessica Kingsley Publishers.

Senge, P. M. (2006) *The Fifth Discipline: The Art and Practice of the Learning Organisation.* London: Random House Business Publishing.

Shinozaki, M., Kanazawa, M., Kano, M., Endo, Y., Nakaya, N., Hongo, M. and Fukudo, S. (2010) 'Effect of autogenic training on general improvement in patients with irritable bowel syndrome: A randomized controlled trial.' *Applied Psychophysiology and Biofeedback 35,* 3, 189–198.

Singer, P. (ed.) (1993) *A Companion to Ethics.* Oxford: Blackwell.

Stokes, J. (2009) 'Institutional Chaos and Personal Stress.' In A. Obholzer and V. Z. Roberts (eds) *The Unconscious at Work: Individual and Organisational Stress in the Human Services.* London: Routledge.

Sue, D. W., Carter, R. T., Casas, J. M., Fouad, N. A. *et al.* (1998) *Multicultural Counseling Competencies: Individual and Organizational Development.* Thousand Oaks, CA: Sage.

SWRB (2010) 'Building a safe and confident future: One year on: Developing a coherent and effective framework for the continuing professional development of social workers.' Available at https://www.education.gov.uk/publications/eOrderingDownload/4%20Principles%20for%20a%20CPD%20framework.pdf, accessed 16 October 2012.

SWRB (2011) 'Professional Capability Framework.' Available at www.collegeofsocialwork.org/pcf.aspx, accessed 16 October 2012.

Tew, J. (2006) 'Understanding power and powerlessness: Towards a framework for emancipatory practice in social work.' *Journal of Social Work 6,* 1, 33–51.

Thomas, L. (1992) 'Racism and Psychotherapy: Working with Racism in the Consulting Room: An Analytical View.' In J. R. Kareem and R. Littlewood (eds) *Intercultural Therapy.* Oxford: Blackwell Scientific.

Thompson, K. (2011) *Therapeutic Journal Writing: An Introduction for Professionals.* London: Jessica Kingsley Publishers.

Thompson, M. (2010) *Understand Ethics.* London: Hodder Education.

Thompson, N. (1995) *Theory and Practice in Health and Social Welfare.* Buckingham: Open University Press.

Thompson, N. (2003) *Promoting Equality.* Basingstoke: Palgrave Macmillan.

Thompson, N. (2007) *Power and Empowerment.* Lyme Regis: Russell House Publishing.

Thompson, N. (2012) *Anti-Discriminatory Practice.* Basingstoke: Palgrave Macmillan.

Thompson, N. and Thompson, S. (2008) *The Social Work Companion.* Basingstoke: Palgrave Macmillan.

Trappe, H.-J. (2010) 'The effects of music on the cardiovascular system and cardiovascular health.' *Heart 96,* 23, 1868–1871.

Wonnacott, J. (2012) *Mastering Supervision.* London: Jessica Kingsley Publishers.

Woodcock, M. (1989) *Team Development Manual.* Aldershot: Gower.

Yan, M. C. (2008) 'Exploring cultural tensions in cross-cultural social work practice.' *Social Work 53,* 4, 317–327.

SUBJECT INDEX

AUTHOR INDEX

Lightning Source UK Ltd.
Milton Keynes UK
UKOW04f0609070716

277788UK00002B/160/P